The Dresden Dolls Companion

In Memory of Beloved
Ben Chappel

Library of Congress Cataloging in Publication Data

Palmer, Amanda 1976-
The Dresden Dolls Companion by Amanda Palmer

1. Music, Popular (Songs, etc.) - United States.
Order No.
ISBN-13: 978-1-5756-0888-4
ISBN-10: 1-57560-888-X
Manufactured in the United States of America.

The Picture Book of Sexual Love

Spring 2005
photo by: Scott Irvine

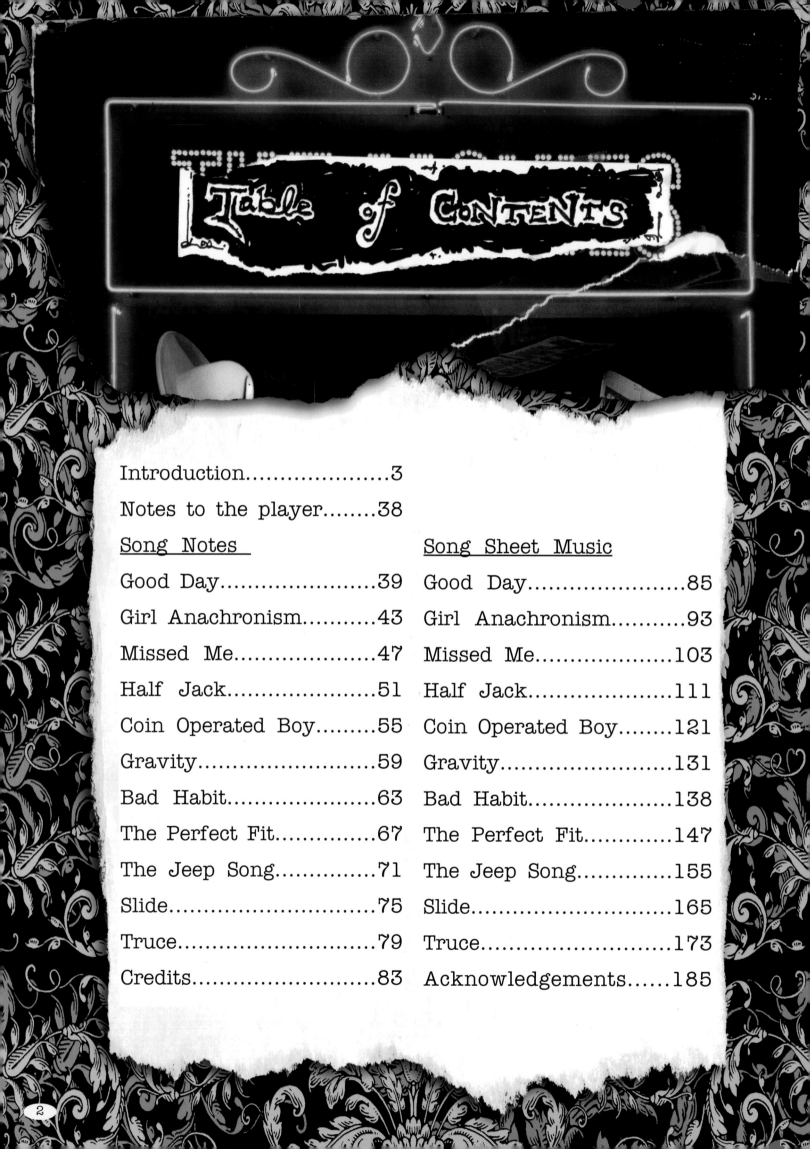

Table of Contents

In the first place

this is not a standard book of sheet music. When I realized a couple of years ago that there was a demand for this, I decided that it would be much more fun and infinitely more fitting to compile a book about the process of making the record rather than a typical sheet-music collection. But I am not, by nature, a finisher of things. My own self-flagellating sense of perfection, coupled with my overwhelming lack of time-management skills, put off its publishing until now. But I'm satisfied. While flipping through the songbooks in the sheet music section of my local record store, I was really unimpressed. Each book was a template of the last, a stock formula, lacking with a few meager exceptions, any personal involvement of the musicians in the creative process of making the book. A photo here or there. Nothing personal. I resolved to develop the kind of book that I would want to buy myself....and moreover, a book that would interest not only our piano or guitar-playing fans, but anybody interested in the band, our process, and the songs themselves. A companion, if you like, written to accompany the record.

The act of writing in paragraphs and full sentences is harrowing. I prefer songs. Lyrics are flexible; terrible grammar is often excused and flights of fancy may wander without fear of being reigned in. Necessary and superfluous details alike are free to follow random tangential tracks. One may safely overuse adjectives and expletives. Exposition, beginning, middle and end, are unnecessary. All of the editing, the reading and then the re-reading . . . it's fucking boring. This sort of writing, this quiet and printed prose, is best left to journalists. It is best left to the people who passionately and properly use words such as "supposition," or "furthermore," or "nevertheless". Nevertheless, I feel like a fraud even attempting it out of necessity, as if I'm holding high some fictitious flag for the "I Am Not Just a Mere Musician, But a Glorious Writer, As Well" guild in the sky, where Jim Morrison and Nick Cave sit around on ratty Edwardian couches discussing Faust and Fitzgerald, drinking whiskey. So, anyway. I will humbly attempt to concoct this little ditty about where our first record came from, and I will hope not to bore my readers to death.

The timing of this book

has worked out very strangely. As I sit here writing this and preparing the artwork and amassing all of the old photographs, we are just finishing up our second record. I come back from the studio with a head full of new stories and sounds, then attempt to faithfully re-capture for you the past. Digging back and trying to re-create those feelings puts our current situation into wild perspective and seems inappropriate, as if I'm reminiscing about an old lover over dinner on a first date. I cannot imagine going through this same process a second time with the sheet music for the new record. These older songs have a particular place in my life and memory because they were written for an imaginary audience. They came into the world not knowing if they would ever be heard. Of course I can't know how other musicians or songwriters feel about their first records, but for me, it's been like losing my virginity: for better or for worse, you can never forget the first time. I daydreamed from the age of thirteen about releasing my first record. For years I decorated endless spiral notebook covers with potential album artwork. I came up with hundreds of perfect album titles each year. When our own first record became a reality, I could barely believe it. Some of the songs had waited almost ten years to be exposed. It was the most frustrating and the most complete act of self-expression I had ever attempted. The recording and mixing of the record itself was a frenzied, furious process that will never be repeated. This recent album recording for our second record had a totally different feeling to it. Not a bad feeling, but a different one. This time around, we walked into the recording studio like another person might walk into work at the office. The first time around we were crazed communists in a fascist country, publishing underground literature in our basements by candlelight. There was an acute sense that every decision we made would be the one to potentially make or break our futures.

On Songs and Songwriting

Each of these songs has a complex story and a complicated history. Each has visuals, twists and turns and explanations. I suppose most songs do. Some musicians and songwriters, however, prefer to protect all their mystery. I do not subscribe to this style of songwriting. One choice I do face, however, is deciding what to reveal and what to exclude. There exist an infinite number of paths I can take when trying to explain a song: what I had to eat the morning I wrote a particular verse, what billboard I passed that morning that inspired that line, what song on the radio kept buzzing in the back of my head until ultimately manifesting itself into my chorus without my conscious knowledge. Such things are often a source of pride but even more often a source of embarrassment. The song "Yesterday," says the lore, started out with Paul McCartney rolling out of bed with the tune in his head. He reached for the piano where he banged the chords and croaked out the first nonsense words that came to him ("Scrambled eggs, oh my darling how I love your legs") and spent the next few days convinced that the song was too classic sounding to be his own invention. He was sure he had someone else's song stuck in his head. His friends assured him otherwise as he sang the tune and waited expectantly to be told that the melody was indeed ripped from an old Cole Porter standard, but the news never came. I do believe, though, that everything is derivative of something else, and that's just the nature of music and of art. So, when a writer chooses to share the pattern and threads that went into making a manuscript, what they choose to reveal about their process is a question of their own personal style. Paul could have chosen to keep that story to himself, but the charming humanity of it makes his song that much more beautiful and the mystery of songwriting that much more difficult to understand. There are so many variables. Why that morning and not some other morning? What if his girlfriend had spent the night? What if he hadn't had a piano in the room?

Usually, ideas for my songs come and go without much effort. On any given day they will appear in their embryonic form, they'll whistle themselves around in my head as I drive, they'll chant to me as I do the dishes or walk down the street. One thing is certain though; they rarely allow themselves seen when there is other music playing. This is why I have happily left the Volvo's stunted stereo in disrepair for four years running. They rarely come when I am engaged with others socially. They peer out from the darkness, timid and tentative, when they think they might receive some attention and consideration. Lately, under the pressure of so much touring, my nascent ideas have become as afraid and unseen as a sad, abused child hiding on the closet floor, tucked behind the winter clothes until he feels safe enough to come out. Even after weeks at home after touring, the creative faucet sometimes refuses to budge, and my mind and body demand to be looked after, fed and watered and taken care of in the wake of non-stop motion, voices, input and time spent in the continuous company of others. It's an irritating refrain, but Ben Franklin's creative ratio of "1% inspiration; 99% perspiration" refuses to be proven untrue.

In the house where I live, we are all plagued by an overabundance of ideas and a sorry yet stereotypical lack of time management skills common amongst artists. We have grown hostile to those around us who dare suggest that they might "have a great idea." Get out," we cry, "We don't need any more fucking ideas!" No, we need more time. We need more resources to finish our own ideas, rotting, untended and malnourished for months or years, stacked upon each other in the figurative or literal closets we keep. Boxes upon boxes overflowing and labeled with sad marker print, "Song Ideas: 1992", "Photos for Website: 1999-2001", "Theatrical Concepts to Change the World". Boxes labeled "Street performance acts" rest on milk crates adorned by signs signifying them as "Short Film Ideas". "Clothes to Turn into Other Clothes" hang beside tacked up "GI Joe Figures for Future Art Projects. The list goes on, the boxes pile up.

The Long Mess of Material

Under my grand piano is a pile of papers. No, maybe a meadow of papers that fills up at least eight square feet. They've been furiously at rest there, stagnant in that state for nearly six months and I'm unsure what's in there. There must be pieces of paper with lyrics to songs that began ten years ago; songs that I am convinced could be quite magnificent if I could only sit down and attend to them. I have found, however, over my many years of songwriting and not-songwriting, that the longer an embryo of an idea sits idle inside a box, the less likely it is to ever find itself born.

The more attention given to it without moving it forward, the more obstinately it refuses to budge. They look up at me in their unfinished blankness and déclassé through lips only half sketched, "We could be great fucking ideas, Amanda, but you won't allow us to be anything more than this." The completion process occurs only through discipline, which is something I have been very good at. It is only through the epic sacrifice of a brilliant idea to a mediocre song that one learns what does and does not work. Letting those embryonic ideas go is a painful process, especially because deep within it lies the fear that the day may someday come when the ideas, be them brilliant or mediocre, stop introducing themselves at all.

Beside the meadow under my piano are two plastic filing boxes, which, in a rare and manic blast of discipline three years ago, I filled with manila folders that I managed to order alphabetically. One box is marked "Finished", the other is marked "Not." The "Finished" box is filled with lyrics and drafts for songs dating back to when I was fifteen. The "Not" box has drafts for songs that are in enough of a finished state to have titles, but will most likely never be completed. I can be honest with myself at this point, and honest, too, with you: surely most of the "Not" songs will never see the light of day. They are just too convinced that they are good ideas. I just went to the bedroom with my digital camera -- I am writing at the kitchen table -- and took a picture of the meadow and the mess for your enjoyment:

old piano

new piano

Then there are the tapes. Tapes and minidisks and DATs that house the even more painful sound recordings of song ideas. I'll go take of picture of some of them, too. I'm beginning to feel as though this may be somehow therapeutic. For good measure, I'll throw in a photo of my feet and four composition books from high school and college, where most of my old songs live.

the 4 composition books
from high school

therapy

Once upon a time I kept a recording Walkman by my piano so that anytime I got an idea, I could record it, then improvise over it to see where it could go. Curse Sony and all those gadget-inventing fuckers. In retrospect, I can see this was my first obstacle as a productive songwriter. At the age of fourteen I was so obsessed with the idea of having a finished product that it was with splendor and ceremony that I heard the clicking stop of the first ninety-minute tape as I finished recording an idea. "I am a legitimate musician," I declared, "I have ninety minutes worth of song ideas." I then ritualistically listened to the whole tape; impressed with myself and my lovely ideas. Then, of course, the tape needed a title.

The ideas, all the unfinished tracks, needed titles. I am amazed that I didn't create full-color artwork to go with these fucking tapes. And thus began an era of archiving my own incompletion.   I captured ideas; rarely finished the songs I began I'd finish a tape, listen, be pleased, title and date, move on to the next. This went on for years. To be fair, I did complete a few songs here and there. But here's the interesting part, and I can't believe I didn't notice it back then.   The songs that became "finished songs" almost never show up on these tapes in a primitive form. They were never recorded ideas. They were born, paid attention to and finished, usually all in one sitting.

My Favorite
Musical Instrument
is

Piano

The perfect example of this is Slide. The idea struck me at home, very late one night. I was fifteen. It was a school night. It started when my brain went off onto a poetic tangent about how a girl falling down a slide would be a perfect metaphor for falling (perhaps willingly) from sexual innocence.   I crept down into the living room, where the piano was; I wasn't allowed to play after my parents went to bed*

And very quietly I played the two chords I had in my head, then went back to my bedroom, took a piece of blank white paper and a thin grey magic marker, lay down on the floor at the foot of my futon, and wrote down all the lyrics at once.   The melody was firmly planted in my memory.   I trusted it would not flee in sleep, and in the morning it was still there. The next day at school, during lunch, I went to the practice rooms and played it for the first time. And then it was done. I went back to tweak a few lyrics over the years, but it has more or less stayed the same as it was the night I wrote it.

And this has been the case with other songs time and time again. The best songs I've ever written have been strictly one- (or maybe two-) sitting affairs. For me, an idea for a song is like a infant. You can't neglect it for a few days, much less a few years, and then come back to the cradle and decide to care again. The damage done is irreversible, often fatal. This is, however, only the way this songwriter works. I have read countless interviews with folks who have a completely different process and approach. I read with electric-green envy the accounts of writing songs on the road (I can't yet), picking up ideas from five years ago and turning them into shiny new songs (I almost never can), writing away from the instrument (seems impossible) and other such feats of songwriter prowess that leave me feeling undisciplined, unorganized and unauthorized to give anybody advice on the subject.   So stop reading if you're looking for advice. I got none. The best I could suggest – if you are a songwriter seeking guidance - is that you breathe free and easy in the knowledge that there is no Perfect System, and like everything else, everyone is just bumbling along, faking it the best they can.   Whatever works, use it.

*typical scenario:
Amanda (mildly dramatized): "I am an Artist! I must be free to create at any hour when inspiration strikes!"
Parents, in perfect unison: "Wonderful dear, but then we can't sleep and we need to work so we can pay the mortgage and eat."
Amanda: "You don't understand me! Fuck you!"

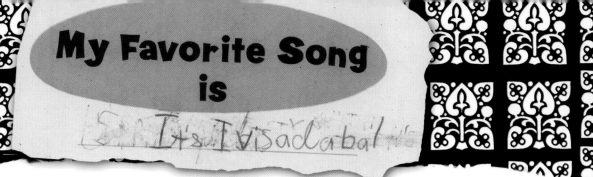
When I was in college, I had something approaching a catholic guilt about my inability to transform ideas into songs. It became obsessive. Why can't I take these ideas and turn them into anything? Why can't I write anything new and actually finish it? I was so infatuated with the stillbirth-nature of my own creativity that I actually created a piece of experimental theater, a one-woman show that ran about an hour, in which I made a audio-collage using what I considered "the best" of hundreds of hours ideas I had recorded. I mixed these together with an interview I conducted with myself after my death. The stage was covered with a sheet and the entire show took place in silhouette from the light of a slide projector that I fed with disturbing photographs of myself and my family. I stripped and simultaneously destroyed 50 or 60 decoy Maxells with a sledgehammer and strung up the unwound magnetic tape on a clothesline, gradually obscuring the entire stage. It was the ultimate in narcissistic performance: a living art testament to my own laziness. It was titled "Potential". I got two school credits (one theater and one music), but my ability to compose songs did not improve. I was a classic College Bullshit Artist.

If you really want to give me a

Birthday Present

here is what
I want most of all.

A ticket to astray cats conse...

Technology was changing and I realized that the using the recording Walkman was horrendously outdated. I tried a bunch of different techniques, from DAT to MiniDisc to iPod with microphone attachment, but ultimately came to the conclusion that the best solution may be to ban myself from recording my ideas entirely. Surely I'll always find myself scratching lyrics onto napkins and dollar bills and dialing my own voicemail, leaving cryptic song messages that will most likely never be tended to again. Perhaps these ideas are happy enough to exist wholly inside their own obscurity. I have been home from tour only two weeks at the time of this writing and haven't felt the urge to record a single idea. No matter; the time will come. The abused kid is locked in the bathroom taking a mindless bath. Soaking up the nothingness. And like a good mother, I will leave the kid alone if he wants to take a fucking bath.

What else?

I collect ___Newspaper-thigns dack fothers.___

ssss

Lately I've been trying to use Technology to my advantage and I sing ideas for songs into my voicemail or email them to myself. Of course, most of these ideas (surprise) never get used, but the ones that seem too good to lose often hang on somewhere in my subconscious, even if I don't record them. Often it's just the act itself of committing an idea to paper (even if the piece of paper winds up wine-soaked and trash-bound) that solidifies it in my memory bank. Once I get the time and discipline to sit down at the piano, it's a process. Once again, I'd be fascinated to see how other songwriters do this, and over time I've found my own idiosyncratic rituals. First, I turn the phone off. I make sure I have plenty of empty paper at both the piano and the kitchen table. I make sure there are felt-tipped pens everywhere within reach (I hate pencil, it smudges, and I hate ballpoint pens with a passion...they stop writing randomly at the most inopportune moments). I then sit at the piano and play the little seed of song and improvise until I have a few sections to play with. I let myself sing nonsense until I discover what's working lyrically - even if the lyrics are total non-sequiturs. For me, one key to songwriting is to let nonsense flow freely. Sometimes your subconscious can work through ideas in ways that your intellectual mind never can and, better yet, can give birth to a phrase or a lyrics that can then be interpreted and molded by your thinking mind. For example, I may begin writing a song with a vague idea for a topic and improvise some nonsense lyrics over some random chord changes. Something will stick out and sound right - sometimes because the rhythm of the words just fits perfectly with the tempo and the chords, sometimes because the words just happen to create a striking image, and I'll take that nonsense phrase and muse about where it could lead and what context I could squeeze it into. Often, a single word and it's natural inflection will write an entire song.

My Favorite Color is

PinkBlackRed

Ritual is Hazardous To Your Health.

Once I have a concrete idea for the song established and some lyrics to clean up, I'll walk over to the kitchen table (it's about nine steps from Piano in the Bedroom to Table in the Kitchen) and sit down to write whatever lyrics have come. Trying to take the essence of what I played and came up with, I'll take the time to mull and expand, which I find difficult to do while sitting at the piano. Mind you, this whole time I am writing only lyrics; I never write down musical notes because - surprise again - I don't know how. Nor do I need to. I memorize as I go along and what I can't memorize, I improvise. Having sat at the table for a chunk of time, I'll get stumped on some section or line and have to go back to piano to road-test what I've written. Often what sounds good in my head while sitting at the table won't fit once I sing it, and so back to the table it is. Once I've gone back and forth a few times, I put a small notebook in my pocket, make sure I have a pen, and walk two blocks to Dunkin Donuts. While there, I order a medium half-decaf half-hazelnut coffee with cream and sugar. I think about The Song, The Whole Song and Nothing But The Song. Sometimes the music in Dunkin Donuts will inspire me. I was in there recently on one of these song-writing half-caffeinating excursions and they were playing "Eternal Flame." No joke. The chord changes got me out of a problem with the song I was working on. I then walk the three blocks to my apartment and try to find Pope to see if he has any cigarettes so I can bum one. If he's not around I look for Lee (the Best Landlord Ever) who is less likely to have cigarettes but you never know. If I can't find Lee I sneak up to his apartment and check his secret cigarette drawer because sometimes there will be a stray American Spirit drying up in there. If I have no luck, I leave my apartment Again, walk to the end of the block, and buy a new pack of cigarettes with the intention of smoking Just One for Inspirational Purposes and giving the rest of the pack away to Pope or Lee. Sometimes I will buy three packages of Cigarettes in one week but smoke a total of four. I quit smoking three years ago. Now, back to the table with coffee and cigarettes in ready position, I sit back down to write more lyrics. I fetch my Brandenburger Tor ashtray from the side of the sink and get a package of matches and light a cigarette thinking about how incredibly weak-willed I am and wondering when I will ever be able to grow up and approach the songwriting process without the Coffee and Cigarette Ritual Crutch.

Some Early Background and The Piano...

The majority of the songs on this record were written between the ages of 22 and 25, Slide being the obvious exception and Bad Habit being the other (I wrote that at 18). I never really learned how to properly play the piano. My education started at age 4 when I hoisted myself up onto the bench of my mother's upright piano and started banging. My mother, Kathy, claims that it sounded very musical. When I turned 5, we moved to a bigger house and my mother hunted for a grand piano that resembled the one she'd played as a child. Finally, through a friend of a friend, I believe, she landed a very good deal on a cheap Steinway grand piano from the turn of the 19th century. I used to work in a piano repair shop and if this atrocity had ever come through the door they would have given it in the oft-repeated diagnosis that befell many these abused old instruments: "This piano needs a new piano". Still, I'll never, ever love a piano the same way. It sounded perfect to me.

The strings were all original and too rusty and stiff to be tuned properly, so the piano was always a whole step below concert pitch. They also had a tendency to break frequently, but I found out in later life (when I bought my first, spanking brand-new piano and within the first 6 months broke four strings) that this was due to my "style" of playing rather than any inadequacy of the piano. It was a wonderful excuse, however ("it's the piano's fault....it's old!"), and my generous mother always paid the repair bill, though sometimes it would take weeks and weeks for a string to get tended to, resulting in some interesting sounds that sometimes even proved inspirational.

When I was 7 or 8 years old, I took a few lessons down the street with a woman who gave group lessons to children in the neighborhood, but I remember very little of that. When I was 12 or so, my mother sent me to a woman on the other side of town. I took the bus there once a week for a couple of years and hated going. I had, unfortunately, already dubbed myself An Artist (I was around 14 at this time) and was pretty sure that these boring piano songs I was trying to learn had nothing to do with what I wanted to achieve in life. I had a good ear, though, and I would entertain myself by playing tapes of classical piano music for a few seconds at a time (pause, stop, rewind, play, pause, stop, rewind) while picking out the notes on the piano. For some reason this seemed infinitely more exciting than learning the foreign language of music notation. If I had found a more creative teacher who had realized that I really wanted to improvise and write, things may have turned out differently. I felt her students were the equivalent of those schoolchildren in Pink Floyd's The Wall, showing up for lessons each week to be brainwashed and doomed to come out the other end of some kind of musical meat-grinder. Even after pleading and begging on the part of my mother (and repeated bribery attempts, some of which worked for a while), I quit. And I can say honestly at this point that though I was thoroughly convinced that I didn't need no musical education, I was actually just lazy and HATED, HATED, HATED practicing the piano. I still do. I avoid practicing at all costs.

1992- the sorry state of things....

So instead, I pounded on the piano, making noise and relishing the sound of one or two chords repeatedly hammered. Without knowing anything about punk (really, I knew Nothing . . . I only remember being grossed out, at age 11, by the fact that a band could be named "The Sex Pistols") I was my own force of punk-rock piano, insisting that sheer volume, speed and passion created a far more noble sound than actual skilled musicianship. But (by way of losing all punk-rock cred), there were a few simple classical pieces I had learned to play by ear or by slow sight-reading, and I played them constantly in an attempt to prove that I COULD play this shit if I really WANTED to, but I DIDN'T WANT TO, so there, and now I will resume my banging thank you very much and I hate you all. Oh 14, I miss you.

The First Songs

And I began writing. What had started out as repetitive improvisations gradually gave birth to songs and I added the best lyrics I could come up with. I assure you, they were awful. I could best describe those early-era songs as a kind of a D-list Cyndi Lauper. Example titles include Scared Little Boy, Waiting For You, Secrets, Reality, Why Did You Leave Me Alone? and You Don't Care About Me. I needn't continue. Suffice it to say that the themes haven't matured much even if the songwriting has. Anyway, my mother, who at this point was impressed by the fact that, despite my lack of skill, I stubbornly intended to continue with my musical self-educating, finally gave it to my pleading. We drove to a scary man's house somewhere in Boston and purchased my first used keyboard: a fifty-dollar Casio CZ-1000 and my first four-track, a Fostex. I owe my mother a lot. She didn't understand anything about modern music equipment. Despite the middle-of-the-night conflicts, she and my step-father supported me in my dream to be a songwriter. They never told me to Give It Up and think about what i REALLY wanted to do when i grew up. I try hard not to take that for granted. I taught myself the fundamentals of four-track recording through trial and error and began recording my first songs. I recorded them live, the keyboard into one track and the vocal into another, occasionally adding my own background vocals. All of these early recordings are downright painful to listen to, because (even if you can appreciate the budding songwriter within) my voice was an off-key, fake-english-accent-ridden, shrieking death-howl. All qualities that I have cleverly honed into what they call "personal style", but in the early stages, I was unlistenable way past the point of being cute. I made my first four-track tape (7 or 8 songs, I think), Xerox artwork colored in with marker, I adopted a stage name (Zonia Wilkes) and it must have been at around that time that I became fully committed to becoming a Rock Star when I grew up. Of course, when asked, I would answer "an actress or maybe a singer", because Rock Star sounded totally pretentious and completely obnoxious.

self-portrait at piano... around 1993   (ANOTHER HOPE)

Then There Was High School...

High School was, if only from a song-writing perspective, a productive time and I found myself in a jazz improv class which was a pride and joy of the school's music department. The class basically consisted of a little theory, a little jazz history, a little listening, a little lecturing, and a lot of playing, all directed by the manic jazz-ringmaster Jeff Leonard, who was also the Band and Orchestra leader. We would jam out and trade solos to standard jazz tunes. Most kids were also taking private lessons and almost all of them were far more proficient at their instruments than I was. I could read the chords charts but not the notes, and though my ear was good my playing wasn't good enough to really keep up, so I spent most of my time embarrassed. But, I learned a great many things and most importantly, I was being exposed to great songs (even if they were being butchered by high school saxophones). The only time I think I really impressed Jeff, who was generally unimpressed by my lazy practice habits, was when I managed to transcribe an entire Thelonius Monk solo (for "Mysterioso") by ear and busted it out during class.

The first week of sophomore year of high school presented a breaking point and I dropped out of school altogether. I just refused to go, and vowed to spend my days in the library, looking up long words and feeling superior, until I figured out what to do. I hated the teachers, hated the classes, hated all the students and was convinced there was a better place for me at some hippy school where Art was God and the students ran festooned with handmade garlands in their hair, paint all over their hands, and eyeliner running down their faces as they leapt, free from the constrictions of "classes" and "homework" through fields of unmown grass. My parents were not into this idea. After a week of heated debate, a few visits to the town psychologist (thank god this was in the days before ADHD was all the rage, I would have been on a Ritalin prescription before you could say "Overmedicated Youth of America") and knock-down, drag-out meetings with the school counselor, it was compromised that I would return to the public High School, drop the classes that I despised most, make up the credits in summer school and be allowed to take two classes of "independent music study" with Jeff Leonard, the jazz teacher. We didn't know quite what these "independent music studies" would entail, but the vague mumbling was that I would be under his charge in the music department wing of the school and would work on "my compositions." It was bribery, and it worked. Jeff kindly agreed and within a few months I realized that the man was so incredibly busy with other things that I could basically do whatever I wanted as long as he occasionally saw me kicking around.

Sometimes I would bug him for a few weeks to hear a new song I had written and he'd eventually make the time. I remember playing him "Slide" right after it was written. His feedback: "It's not too bad . . . I hope someday your musical writing catches up to the sophistication of your lyrics." He was not one to cushion. Nobody else heard my songs, though I was writing a lot. I played things here or there for select friends, but nobody ever knew how to react, nor did they realize how terrified I was to hear what anyone thought of my writing. I was sensitive to the point of paralysis. I spent a lot of time working in the drama department and I was in most of the school musicals and plays (the music director once famously stopped the entire orchestra during a dress rehearsal to storm down the aisle screaming "Amanda!!!! You CAN'T SING!!") and spent most lunches hanging out with myself in the practice rooms, playing whatever I was working on. I avoided people like the plague, spending much of my life with headphones and sunglasses on listening to The Legendary Pink Dots and seeing music videos in my head.

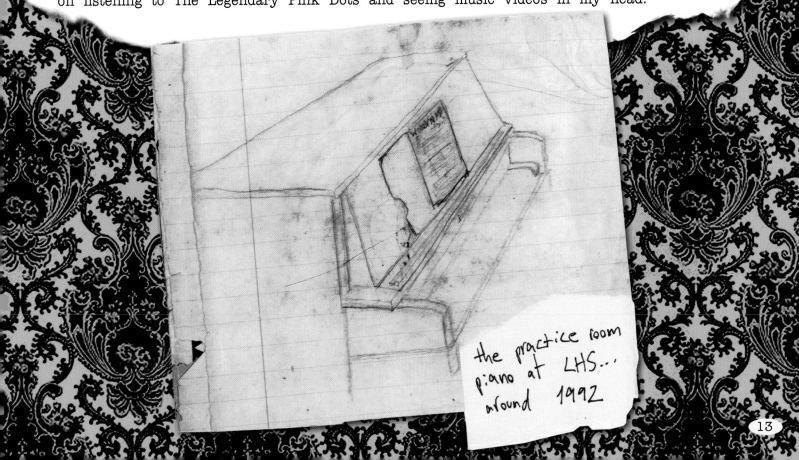

the practice room piano at LHS... around 1992

My senior year, the musical was "Carousel" (a complete piece of shit Rogers and Hammerstein schlock musical) and I was really disgusted at some of the content. There was literally a song called "What's The Use of Wondering" in which the protagonist explains, to her girlfriends, that it's not important if your husband beats you senseless. What's important is that you love him, and you will stand by him or face The Wrath. I was really sickened. So I wrote a dark protest song, called "June Is Busting Out All Over" (the title was lifted from another Carousel song about the birds n' bees and what happens in the spring to ALL species). Sample lyrics: "The pain is dull/it's something like/a wet electric shock/but he's your fella/and you love him/and all the rest is talk". I took a chance and played it for the director, Steve Bogart, who was one of my heroes and one of the few adults I liked and trusted. He hated the musical too (he was forced to do it due to some retiring teacher who picked it) and he loved the song, and suggested that I sing it during the intermission. And so it was then that I gave my first public performance of one of my songs. The best part was my costume . . . since the big clambake scene was right after intermission, I delivered the song in a yellow gingham dress wearing a matching shawl and a straw hat with ribbons on it. It was Perfect.

I was also in one band in high school, for about a month. We called ourselves "Fear of Muzak" and had three rehearsals but never played a show. Our songs consisted of covers by The Cure and New Order . . . and we wrote one original called "Disco Ain't Dead." I played Casio Synthesizer. It was 1993. We rehearsed in my living room, and one day I asked the three other guys in the band how they felt about wearing make-up. They all agreed that it was a Proper Rock Star Thing To Do, and I yelped and ran, heart racing and soul bursting, to the bathroom where I gathered all of my lipsticks and eyeliners and just went to town on the poor guys. When I was done, they all looked like Robert Smith after a night of serious drinking. A sure sign of Things to Come.

And Then College and Stewing....

Then things took a turn for the worse. College yielded a blank sonic canvas. Try as I might, I could not adjust to life without my own piano and privacy. Countless hours in college practice rooms, friend's basements, churches and other random places yielded nothing. The year I lived in Germany (1996, as an exchange student) was especially fruitless and pianoless. I would try to find them here and there, and the results were mostly dismal. I had a job in a small theater in Cologne, and the minute they gave me a key I secretly let myself back into the building at midnight, excited about the prospect of being able to practice every night for months to my hearts content. Within the first few joyous moments of unabashed banging I was met by the wrathful German hollering of Wolfgang, one of the theater's repertory actors, who came storming down in his bathrobe assuring me I would be fired . Unbeknownst to me, he was homeless and sleeping in the theater's offices on a pull-out sofa. He smoked (I am not kidding) upwards of 110 cigarettes a day. Anyway, my key was repossessed but I was not fired. I was also politely asked "to please refrain" from playing the pianos in several piano showrooms. It was fucking depressing. I drank and drank, gained twenty pounds, and bought an accordion. But it was no use, I needed a piano.

VARIOUS SELF-PORTRAITS FROM THE UNHAPPY HIGH SCHOOL & COLLEGE ERA

I did have a wonderful classical teacher for a few years at Wesleyan University named Sanda Schuldmann. She tried her best to instruct me in the ways of Chopin, Beethoven and Scriabin, and I would try to practice, but I often felt like an 18-year-old trying to learn to read children's books. The practice rooms at Wesleyan were in a dark long basement hall and there I would sit, surrounded on all sides by the sounds and scales and flourishes of what I assumed were Real Musicians Practicing Diligently, biting my nails and wondering why I couldn't be More Like Them. My ear was wonderful but my sight-reading skills were atrocious. I would learn a few bars and have them immediately memorized, and so I never learned to actually read music while looking at a page. I could only memorize sounds and hand patterns. To this day, I still need to look at my hands frequently while I play. I also cannot touch-type.

self-portrait (with auto-timer) in wesleyan practice room, around 1994

I would bring my folder of song-notes, day after day after week after year, into those practice rooms, but it was like trying to pull out non-existent teeth. I would stare at half-finished songs and have nothing to add....I was just dry, confused and miserable. Not the kind of miserable that writes angry songs about it, the other kind. The kind that stews about it, silently.

First Real Show

I played my First Real Show at a little space at Wesleyan called The Russell House. It was the spring of my freshman year and I was 18. I prepared for months, selected the songs with terror, and broke out in nightsweats for two weeks leading up to the concert. I made my own flyers and hung them around campus. I had no idea what it would be like or what people would make of me, but I knew that if I was going to be a performing musician, I had to start doing this. The day came and about 20 or 30 curious people showed up. I sat down, took a very deep breath, and played for about an hour. The reaction was generally shocked, but good. I heard a lot of "Jesus, Amanda . . . I didn't know. . . "Didn't know what? That I was so twisted? That I could actually play the piano? I'll never know.

Amanda Palmer

•Senior Antithesis Concert

Original songs for piano and voice   May 13 8pm $5 suggested donation

At the Buttonwood Tree   605 Main Street   Middletown

FAREWELL.

Flyer for my final show during College... self-portrait photo with fire photoshopping by Conor Fahey. (that's Wesleyan burning, by the way.)

Amanda Palmer • Wed, 5/13, 8 pm
Amanda Palmer has never been able to describe adequately the songs she composes and performs for piano and voice, but she usually uses a combination of the words "dirge", "self-indulgent", "melodic", "percussive", "offensive" and "dark" (and, I would add "honest" - ed.). She sings of childhood woes, stupid fraternity boys, finger-picking and dead people. She penned the anti-Starbucks theme song. I suppose it would be fair to consider this performance her anti-thesis for graduation from Wesleyan Univ.

original music   13

12

8 PM $5.00   8
Amanda Palmer   J
it might be dark, offensive   a
and melodic — it works   li
(piano and voice)   m

I played little solo shows every six months or so at college and booked a few at local cafes while I was living in Germany. They were always anxiety-ridden and listening back to the ones I recorded, I can hear that I was quite an amateur performer . . . but I was growing.

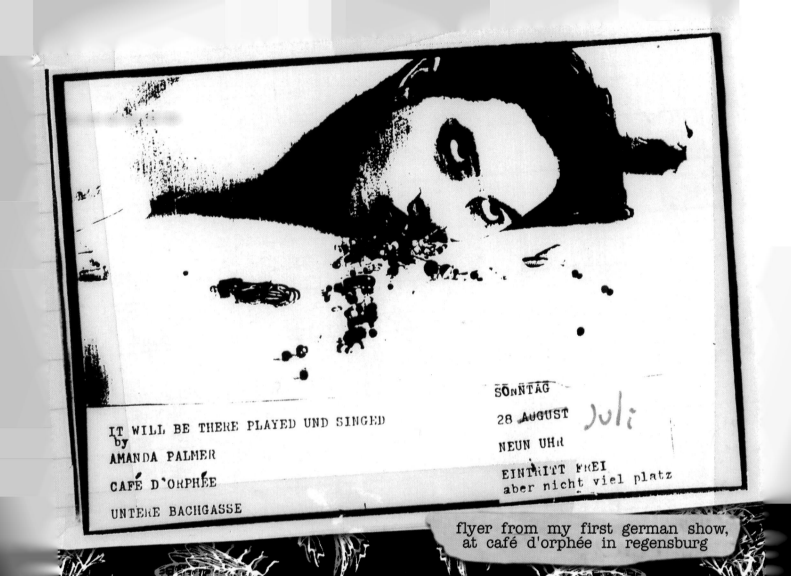

IT WILL BE THERE PLAYED UND SINGED
by
AMANDA PALMER

CAFÉ D'ORPHÉE

UNTERE BACHGASSE

SONNTAG

28 AUGUST Juli

NEUN UHR

EINTRITT FREI
aber nicht viel platz

flyer from my first german show,
at café d'orphée in regensburg

Escaped from College, Amanda Starts To Write

ter college I moved into an apartment in Somerville, MA, and bought a cheap upright. It
s in this apartment that I wrote "Half Jack" and "Girl Anachronism." I was working as a
eet performer and keeping odd hours, so usually I'd write during the day while nobody
s around. I played a few solo shows in local galleries and clubs and started hunting for a
nd. But finding a band for this kind of music was hard, and I was far from being social.
layed (SOME) shows with my cello-playing boyfriend Jonah Sacks (who ended up playing
o on the recording of "Truce") and we played one full-band show with a local drummer
ad found named Martin Bernert under the name "Amanda Palmer and The Void." We blew
the gallery's PA speakers. That was our last show. Soon after, Jonah and I broke up
odbye, cellist) and I was back on my own, hunting for a band. I auditioned a few
mmers, but they all sounded very rock and basic and didn't turn me on.

nding The Cloud Club & Brian

ind that time I discovered and moved into the Cloud Club, the artists' collective where I
live. Words cannot do this place justice. Lee bought the houses in the 70's and have
transformed them into an artistic paradise of strangely-shaped windows, walls, mirrors,
ts and antique eye-candy galore. Walking in the front door, I felt as if a Gaudi building
exploded in Wonderland and a vintage thrift-store on the Lower East side was selling
remnants. There was a geodesic glass dome built onto the roof and magic in the cracks
very wall. I was walking into a dream...here was a place where I could play piano until
in the morning and actually be congratulated by my upstairs neighbor the next day.

The rent was benevolently cheap and I didn't have to struggle to work lots of hours. My musical life, and life in general, began to change rapidly for the better. There was an old spinet piano in the attic and I soon inherited an old grand piano from a kind friend, which was moved into my second story room through the window with a Big Crane. It was around this time, in the fall of 2000, that I met Brian on that fateful Halloween night. I threw a huge salon-style art party at the house and Brian was dragged over by our mutual friend Shawn Setaro (who ended up playing bass on the record). There was a night of entertainment, poets, dancers, performance art and bands, and at around midnight I sat down at the attic spinet to play five or six songs. I think I played Slide, Sex Changes, Girl Anachronism, Half Jack and Kaledrina. Brian sat watching and maintains to this day that he saw his future flash before his eyes. I finished my set. I was dressed, by the way, as a temporary office worker (the irony at that time in my life was striking, believe me....i nailed the costume right down to the little hoopy earrings and the hair scrunchy) and many drinks were drunk. I was sitting on the stairs outside my apartment, drunkenly and excitedly blabbing with three local musicians who were also taken with my set. One played bass, one played guitar and I remember thinking "This is it! I'm going to find my band!!!"

earlier at the same party... brian at the piano, watching poet Sebastian Lockwood tear it up

playing solo on the fateful night

(Ironically, I got together with this bass player a few days later and he had created a terrible dance version of "Half Jack" on his computer. I fled in terror.) Brian, dressed as a severed head in white face, was characteristically sober and observant. He came up at the end of the night and gave me his number. "I really like your songs. I'm a drummer. We should jam." I was still reeling from the excitement about the bass and guitar players, and it barely registered. A week later Brian and I met at his band's rehearsal space. I seem to have conveniently forgotten this part, but Brian claims that I completely spaced our first meeting and it just narrowly worked out, because I happened to pass him in my car as he was leaving my house on his skateboard. Given my history, this is probable. We hauled my keyboard down to his band's practice space and set it up across from his drum set. I played "Sex Changes" and he began to play along. According to Brian I stopped halfway through and looked up at him with a strange look on my face. "What? What? Is it not good" he asked. "No, no...I think...I can tell this is going to work." Within five hours we were best friends, screaming at the tops of our lungs that we were a band (literally, we jumped up and down screaming, "WE'RE A BAND!!! WE'RE A BAAAANND!!!!", and sacrificing and devouring a celebratory apple pie with our bare hands that Brian had stolen from his day-job bakery. It was a beautiful night. Soon after that, I started coming up with band names. Early possibilities were The Left, Finishing School and The Dresden Arms. I wound up at The Dresden Dolls after a brainstorming phone session with my friend Anthony. I thought it was an ideal name to capture the fractured beauty and lost-innocence feeling of the music. I always pictured a little Dresden china doll lying in a pile of firebombed rubble.

Early Doll Days

Things started to happen. Brian quit the other band (where he was an unhappily Indentured Bassist, having been kicked off the drums for political reasons) and we started rehearsing in my bedroom. It was also around this time that I dated and broke up with The Actor, which gave birth, in quick succession, to Boston, Good Day, The Jeep Song, Colorblind and Truce. Meeting Brian inspired me to finish songs, because instead of just letting the ideas lie dormant, I would bring them to him as I wrote and get the instant gratification of hearing a fully finished product. I played him the basic structure of the song and he'd experiment with drum parts while I listened, offering my feedback here or there, mostly dumbstruck and in awe of how perfectly he was in tune with my writing. I barely needed to make a suggestion. He already knew what I had heard in my head, he already knew what to play before I asked. It was a miracle. We had a cellist join the band for a heartbeat, and I had flyers made up proclaiming "Duo seeking guitarist/bassist cellist" that managed to never get taken to the copy shop for a few years running. I think we just knew we had the perfect combination, and weren't in any hurry to mess with it.

rock love after a show in cambridge, MA, 2001

brian vogue-ing during rehearsal in amanda's bedroom

In the spring of 2003, we took on a bass player (Jim Smith, then Andrew DiMola) and a guitarist (Greg Disterhoft) and they joined us on songs like Gravity and Good Day. They sounded great, but we learned the lesson quickly. Less was more and we felt more powerful as a duo, so we dropped the band and pressed on.

We started booking shows left and right and gathering a freaky but devoted fanbase in Boston. A top priority, of course, was to get a recording of some of our songs committed to tape as soon as possible and I turned to my old high-school pal Owen Curtin to help us out. Owen was working at Emerson College as an engineer and had access to their radio station's state-of-the-art studio free of charge, so we went in there and recorded our first five-song demo. As things turned out, we wound up selling this hand-made CD at shows for a year while we worked on a full-on record. It included rough versions of "Half Jack," "Girl Anachronism," "The Perfect Fit," "Colorblind" and "Good Day" and the artwork was a quick-and-dirty xerox collage of paper dolls that I put together in the copy shop. Both Brian and I (mostly Brian, god bless his soul) spent countless hours sitting on my kitchen floor with the CD-duper we decided to purchase, dubbing the demo and xeroxing and hand-cutting the covers so we could sell them at our early shows and online through our rudimentary website. We were both still working, since the band was barely making any money, and our lives were a manic frenzy of odd jobs, shows, short tours and all-night general-band-work sessions (we had no management or help in those days) which bonded us together like epoxy.

the Dresden Dolls are:
amanda palmer : piano & vocals
brian viglione : drums, acoustic guitar, bass

all songs written by amanda palmer
recorded and engineered by owen curtin
mastered by noah blumenson-cook

all songs copyright 2001 amanda palmer

thanks to lee, anthony, kathy & john,
ma & pa viglione and elchael palmer

additional guitar on "good day": brian knoth

www.dresdendolls.com
booking/contact amanda palmer
amanda@brainwashed.com
617

half jack
girl anachronism
the perfect fit
colorblind
good day

Front and back cover art for the first 5-song demo

Finding Martin & Song Selection

We needed to record a real record. We ached. We considered doing our full-length with Owen, but he was a young producer with limited experience and we were hoping to find someone more seasoned to work with and then magically, Martin Happened. It was the summer of 2001 and my friend Marisa called me from New York, where she was hanging out. "You've got to come here. The guy from King Missile is here and the guy from the Swans is recording an album here. Have you ever heard of Martin Bisi? He has a studio in our building." I did some research and found out he had worked with Sonic Youth, Swans (one of my high school favorites), Come, Ornette Coleman . . . after I picked my jaw off the floor, I booked it down there. The place where she was crashing was actually a network of factory buildings attached by a courtyard. Called "The Old American Can Factory", it was an artists'/industrial paradise of activity run by a kindly and super-networked landlord and architect named Nathan. Marisa was helping him with various projects for the summer and I made myself available to help out with whatever was needed. There was a huge event being thrown that week called "FireScape", in which the courtyard was transformed into a vaudevillian club and bands and performance artists surrounded everything. It was truly magical...I helped tend bar and wandered around in a state of glee and then BANG bumped into Martin Bisi. We started talking and within a few days I'd made up my mind: this was The Man for the record. It was more than a year later that we actually began. We had hoped to start in the spring of 2002 but I was having terrible pains in my arms due to over-typing at the keyboard (I was a maniac back then, typing hundreds of emails a day regarding the band) and so we pushed the recording to the fall of 2002. This is the actual list that Brian and I came up with and sent to Martin to start the pre-production process:

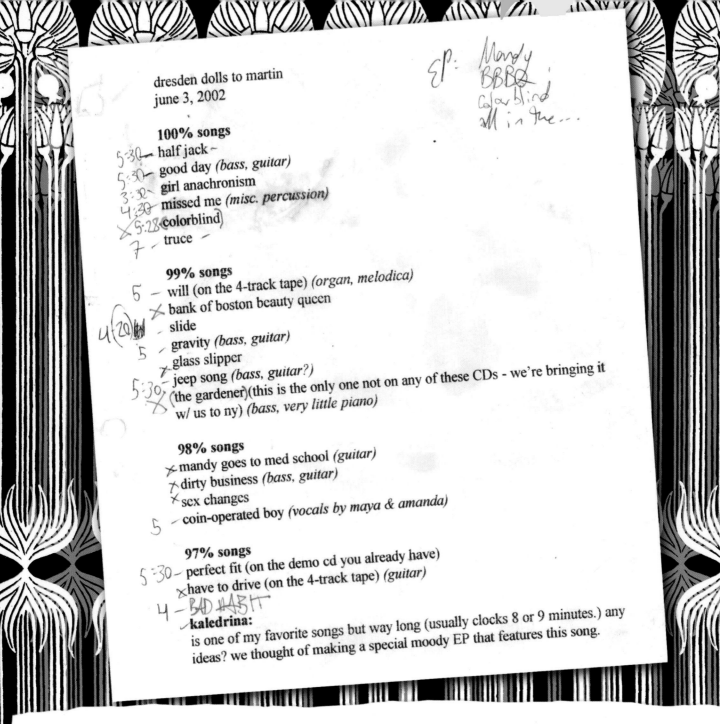

dresden dolls to martin
june 3, 2002

EP: Mandy
BBBQ;
Colorblind
all in the...

100% songs

5:30 — half jack —
5:30 — good day *(bass, guitar)*
3:30 — girl anachronism
4:30 — missed me *(misc. percussion)*
✗ 5:28 colorblind
7 — truce —

99% songs

5 — will (on the 4-track tape) *(organ, melodica)*
✗ bank of boston beauty queen
4 (20) — slide
5 — gravity *(bass, guitar)*
— glass slipper
✗ jeep song *(bass, guitar?)*
5:30 ✗ the gardener (this is the only one not on any of these CDs - we're bringing it
w/ us to ny) *(bass, very little piano)*

98% songs

✗ mandy goes to med school *(guitar)*
✗ dirty business *(bass, guitar)*
✗ sex changes
5 — coin-operated boy *(vocals by maya & amanda)*

97% songs

5:30 — perfect fit (on the demo cd you already have)
✗ have to drive (on the 4-track tape) *(guitar)*
4 — BAD HABIT

kaledrina:
is one of my favorite songs but way long (usually clocks 8 or 9 minutes.) any
ideas? we thought of making a special moody EP that features this song.

Looking back at this is surreal. Coin-Operated Boy was considered a joke-song back then so we figured it wouldn't fit on the record (later, it would turn into the most successful single on the album). Maya - misspelled, her name is Maia - was Brian's 13-year old sister, and we thought it would be brilliant to get her to do the vocal. I can't remember why that didn't happen, but it didn't. I think she had school. Colorblind didn't make it on the record, neither did Will (we recorded it, but cut it at the last minute, putting it instead on the "A is For Accident" live collection), Glass Slipper got vetoed by Martin, as did Gardener. Bank of Boston Beauty Queen didn't make the cut, either. Mandy, Dirty Business and Sex Changes all got axed but are (at the time of this writing) going to show up on our second album. And Perfect Fit, which was way at the bottom, got on the record. The only song missing from this list is Bad Habit, which I didn't consider for the record in the first place. Martin heard it on my old solo demo tape, which I had mailed to him, and he loved it. Brian agreed . . . so I relented. I hadn't wanted to put it on because the content felt too young...a relic of the super-angsty-Amanda era. I was overruled by the two of them, and not one bit sorry.

The Recording Process & Saint Martin

Whether to use digital keyboard or piano was one of the first questions addressed, and I insisted that we record everything on an acoustic piano, preferably a grand. Looking back, I'm not sure that was necessarily the best decision. Brian and I were settled into our habits and sounds using the Kurzweil. I refused to believe that the songs might be better captured by the keyboard, or by cutting the basics with the Kurzweil and overdubbing the acoustic (which is what we did for many of the faster songs on the second record). Anyway, the hunt for a piano was long and arduous. It was way out of our budget to rent one, especially since the NYC rental prices were out of control...on the order of thousands of dollars a week, but we finally persuaded Bradford Reed (the Guy from King Missile who also lived in the building) to loan us his precious family heirloom Steinway, which usually lived in the middle of his huge loft next door to Martin's. We paid to have it moved down to Martin's and gave it back a few weeks later, with Minimal Damage (only one broken-then-fixed hammer and a few replaced strings).

Traveling in my faithful blue Volvo, which was double-nicknamed "Old Blue" (Brian's) and alternately "The Vulva" (Amanda's), we began making the first of many journeys from Boston down to Martin's place in Brooklyn. We drove a few times for initial meetings and pre-production, but Martin and I did the majority of the song-selecting and general attack-planning over the phone. Finally, in September of 2002, we packed The Vulva/Old Blue up with drums and Kurzweil keyboard and headed to Brooklyn for the first round of recording.

Martin's joint was a huge chunk of factory divided into recording space and a large control room. The actual recording area was a huge, cavernous factory basement with giant stone walls and an oppressive atmosphere despite the huge, vaulted ceilings. When we got there it was raging hot and filled with mosquitos and as soon as fall hit, it was Artic. The control room was above the studio and was connected by huge set of fire-escape-style stairs. The control room, where we ended up spending hundreds of hours mixing the record as well, was comfy and sort of like the Brady den, with a huge brown cushion-y couch that was ideal for fort-making. We often amused ourselves by imagining Michael Gira – one of our musical heroes and the Very Serious singer of Swans – making an impenetrable couch fort during mixing. Brian did an excellent imitation of Gira's suspicious eyes peeking out from between two cushions, while his muffled voice would demand more reverb on the guitar.

The coffee-maker was usually gurgling and being manically refilled by Martin (who drank, I kid you not, around 8 cups a day) and the walls were covered with album artwork from all of Martin's many past projects. The Boredoms, Swans, Herbie Hancock, Bill Laswell, John Zorn, Clem Snide . . . countless interesting album covers for our eyes to soak in while our ears had other work to do. I memorized a lot of that artwork by default, the same way you memorize the pictures in your childhood dentist's office while the fluoride is soaking in.

We set up downstairs in two separate rooms connected by a stone arched doorways which Martin covered with Plexiglas for sonic separation. The first day was spent setting everything up, getting drum sounds, experimenting with microphone placement for the piano (I think Martin ended up using 6 different mics, some right on the piano and one room mic at least 20 feet away, for ambience) and the next day we decided to start in with "Good Day". I remember going out to the courtyard, which was the entrance to Martin's studio, and sitting on the metal stairs overlooking the parking lot, thinking to myself "This is it. We're going to record. Holy shit." I took a deep breath, went inside and told the guys I was ready, and we sat down and banged it out. I think we got that one on the second or third take.

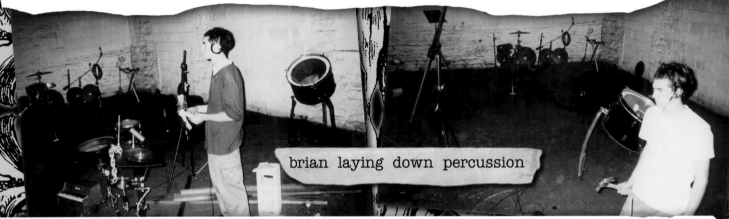

brian laying down percussion

Basic Tracks

We recorded the basic tracks (just piano and drums) for three or four days straight. We didn't record the vocals live because the sound of my voice would have been picked up by the piano microphones. This would have tied the piano and vocal together and been a pain in the ass during mixing, also making it impossible to fix any little piano mistakes or re-take the vocal if I didn't get everything in one shot (which I rarely did). The only song, which is not a single piano-and-drums take is "Missed Me", for which we used the first half of one take and the second half of another. Having come from the land of ProTools with Owen, where everything is edited on computer, it was absolute magic when Martin took the magnetic tape off the two-inch reel, cut it with a razor, and taped the two takes together. It seemed historic. The entire album was recorded onto two-inch tape and then mixed down to half-inch before we took it in for mastering.

On the whole, recording was an infuriating process, and being a perfectionist didn't help. Just the thought that "This is Forever, Maybe" when the tape started rolling was enough to drive me crazy. I tried to be Zen, I tried to just play. It was hard as hell. Brian and I are sometimes on, sometimes not. But time was ticking, there was no way to put it down and do it next week. Everything had to be done Now and so we just played as well as we could and prayed. Martin was a miracle in the studio.

martin and brian
in the drum room

amanda at bradford's steinway
laying basic tracks

the control room

He made occasional comments and suggestions about how to deliver a line or a verse, but mostly he worked with what I gave him and tried to capture without changing too much. He had a few moments of total departure and brilliance; the vocal effect on Gravity was his idea, for example, as was the bluesy piano hook (previously, there had just been chords there). He worked tirelessly and Brian and I marveled at his stamina . . . he just worked and worked and worked until a mix was done. When we got the end of our original deadline and the record was only half-mixed, he practically gave his time to us free so that we could finish. Saint Martin.

where the drums went

Mixing and Mastering

After the basics were ready we started to mix and cut vocals at the same time. Thus began the long and hard era of trekking back and forth between Boston and Brooklyn almost every week. We were gigging and working in Boston (rent still had to be paid) and Martin had a steady stream of other clients, so there was a mind-boggling schedule tetris. I think we determined, at the end, that we drove between Boston and Brooklyn a total of 20 times (about 5 hours each way . . . 4 if we sped and 8 if there was traffic). Martin generally set the schedule and we would start the day at around noon and often work until long after midnight. When we got down to the final hours of a mix, Martin would play us the song and we'd make notes with last minute fixes and changes. Then he'd make adjustments and we'd listen again. Sometimes this process was repeated 6 times, and I'm surprised Martin didn't kill me outright (I began a lot of sentences with "Don't strangle me, but there's One More Little Thing..."). Here's a page of my journal that I used for notes on Good Day. I created my own shorthand because I needed to listen carefully for all the changes without constantly stopping the song. These particular notes, and most others, were about the vocal levels and lyrics I felt were sticking out too much or getting buried by the drums or piano.

piano and vocal land

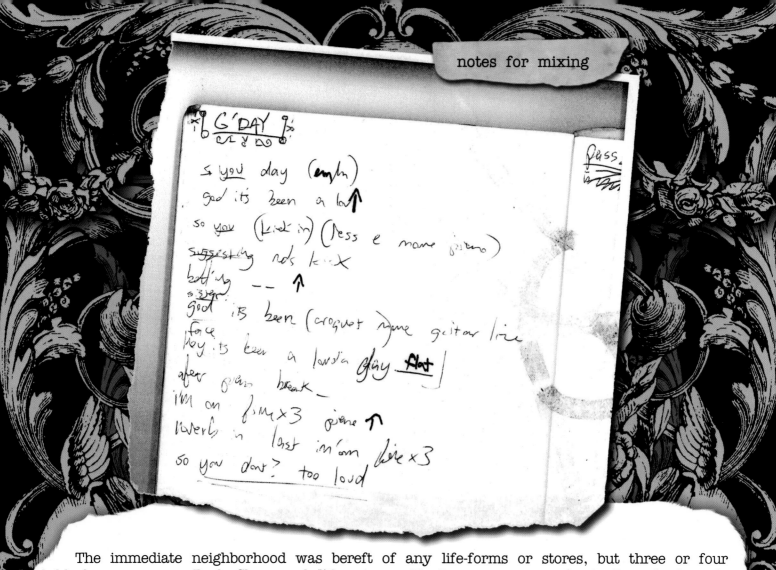

The immediate neighborhood was bereft of any life-forms or stores, but three or four blocks away was Park Slope and 7th Ave with its many moms & strollers & dogs & shops. Every morning Brian and I would ritually stroll our way over to the same muffin and juice store and try to get a little life and air into our lungs before cooping ourselves up for the day. The Tea Lounge on 7th was our favorite destination for breaks and walks and we started treating it like a second home. I knew Stephen Merritt (of the Magnetic Fields) lived around there and I always fantasized I would run into him and we would bond over tea and music. (It never happened).

The days all blurred together. Mixing, vocals, overdubs, mixing. I would do a few vocal takes, Martin and I would listen back and then we'd piece together the vocal. We often used bits from four takes for one finished product . . . and even then we would slip in some word or note that I just hadn't hit in any of the takes. This was all done using the ancient punch-in technique, no computers. No auto-tune, no tricks. Martin was the punch master. We did the same thing with extra piano parts and overdubs. On a typical day, we'd finish vocals and then call Brian, who would be tooling around somewhere, and we'd start mixing. Martin would usually take a few hours to get the song into rough shape and then we would listen and listen and listen. Louder here. Softer there. Kill that altogether. Bring up the bass. Louder. Louder. Louder. Conflicts of opinion and arguments abounded and Brian and I practically killed each other on three or four occasions. Rock n' Roll. There was a real sense of power-struggle. I had a very protective vision for the way I wanted the songs to sound. Brian also had his specific ideas of how to approach things. Often we agreed, but when we didn't, it was every man for himself. I took the stance that the songwriter should get ultimate veto power if it came down to a black and white issue, and this drove Brian crazy. In retrospect, we were suffering from a deficiency of communication skills and the kind of mutual respect we have for each other these days. Martin wasn't the sort of producer who would break up a fight unless it got completely immature; he tended to let us have it out without interjecting. When it came down to it, though, Martin was incredibly diplomatic and we never got too hung-up on a particular part.

This was no "residential studio", but Martin did let us crash there until we outstayed our welcome, at which point we couch-surfed in various parts of Brooklyn and New Jersey. Sometimes I slept in a different bed every night for a week. My favorite haven was Josh and Alina's apartment in Hoboken, where I frequently went to re-coup while Brian went to his Dad's place in the Jersey suburbs. I was the best man at their wedding (Eugene Mirman, stand-up comic extraordinaire, was the maid of honor), and they are two of my dearest friends and confidants. I'd show up after a long day of mixing and singing, exhausted beyond what I thought was humanly possible and literally collapse in a heap on their couch, unable to brush my teeth or make intelligent conversation. One night I fell dead asleep in their bathtub and woke up a few hours later. Alina was working on her own music (Alina Simone, look her up) and we would talk and drink tea and bond about band drama. When we got the absolutely finished copy of the album, we rushed it over to Hoboken and played it for Josh and Alina on their clock-radio CD player. We all fit on one futon. The CD was deemed officially Good.

Mastering took place in Manhattan with Fred Kervorkian at a super-slick-uppity-and-real mastering studio called Absolute Audio. We went in two days in a row and mostly observed as Martin and Fred, who had worked together on lots of records, talked the secret language of sound and got very nitty-gritty about the nuances of basses and trebles and so forth. The excitement was palpable, we were hours away from finally having a finished product and we were bouncing off of the walls.

amanda and brian and the magic shark at Absolute Audio
photo: Martin Bisi

Picking a Song Order

It was in that lounge, over countless coffees and cigarettes on Day Two, that I sat agonizing over the song order. Martin and Brian chimed in with ideas, but no order seemed perfect. I tore my hair out for an hour and half while everybody started to get impatient and finally handed it over to Martin and Fred. These notes are Xeroxed from my journal.

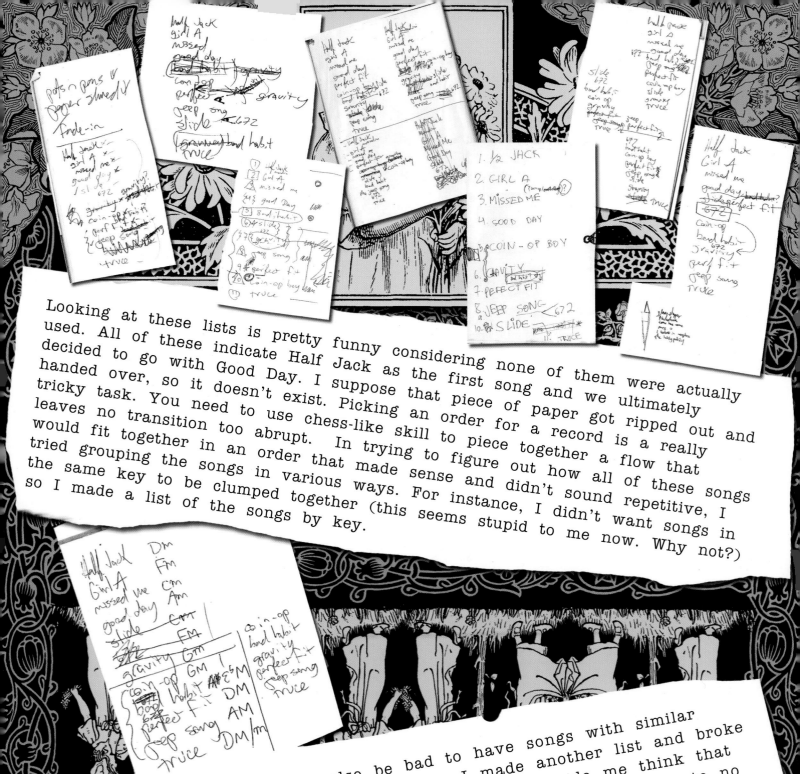

Looking at these lists is pretty funny considering none of them were actually used. All of these indicate Half Jack as the first song and we ultimately decided to go with Good Day. I suppose that piece of paper got ripped out and handed over, so it doesn't exist. Picking an order for a record is a really tricky task. You need to use chess-like skill to piece together a flow that leaves no transition too abrupt. In trying to figure out how all of these songs would fit together in an order that made sense and didn't sound repetitive, I tried grouping the songs in various ways. For instance, I didn't want songs in the same key to be clumped together (this seems stupid to me now. Why not?) so I made a list of the songs by key.

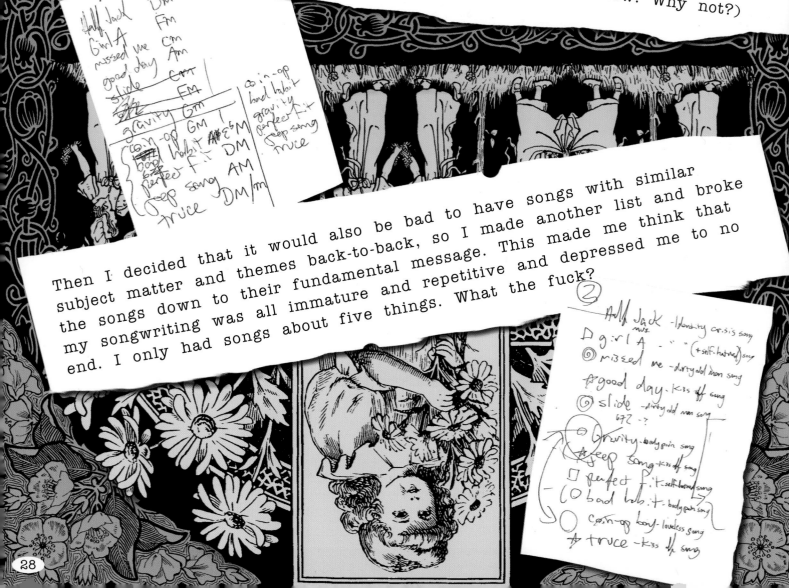

Then I decided that it would also be bad to have songs with similar subject matter and themes back-to-back, so I made another list and broke the songs down to their fundamental message. This made me think that my songwriting was all immature and repetitive and depressed me to no end. I only had songs about five things. What the fuck?

Creating the Artwork

When the record was in its embryonic stages (just as we were beginning to travel a lot down to Brooklyn and put down basic tracks) we asked our wonderful artist friend Veronique D'Entrement to assemble some album artwork using the lyrics. I gave her the dollhouse books and she went to work scanning and setting the lyrics in empty spaces, but these never got used (this page included Will, which didn't end up on the album).

V-Rock's unused layout

Meanwhile, back at the Cloud Club, Michael Pope (our much loved film director, who shot our first two videos and DVD) was living on the first floor underneath my apartment, and Zea and the Martin Brothers (Steve and Thom) were living next door. Pope was working on Neovoxer (his feature film) and the Martin Brothers were helping us put together our website, which was a painstaking process. Thom would pull long hours putting together the design and content, and when we saw how much ass he was kicking we asked if he would help create the album artwork.

We had done a few photo shoots by then and our favorites by far were from a session with Lisa Gordon. We hauled a cabaret table out to the shore near my house and Lisa shot three or four rolls. We poured the wine for theatrical effect only, but I ended up drinking it. Drinking during the day always makes me feel dizzy. You can see the effect this had on the photo shoot after time wore on . . .

Photo shoot out takes
photos: Lisa Gordon

We picked the photo on the album cover because it seemed to have the perfect combination of everything. The airport was only a mile away and so planes were flying overhead the entire time. The plane in the picture, however is a forgery. We imported it from a different shot taken about a minute later. Here's the Real Plane.

Real Plane for Album art
photo: Lisa Gordon

Final Album shot
photo: Lisa Gordon

As soon as we had Record in Hand, I started making little promo CDs using our CD-burner and sending them out to every person I could think of who might help out. I basically followed two paths at once; I was trying to land us a record deal but I kept the solid back-up plan of self-releasing the record if nothing happened. Here is the History of the Promo CD, as Thom and I worked to get the cover finished:

-history of promo CD-

The rest of the artwork just came together organically. I knew I wanted to use a Digipak (a cardboard case instead of traditional jewel case) and so I started thinking in terms of panels and how we could keep the art balanced and symmetrical. Thom and I spent many late nights photoshopping at the Cloud Club. He had endless patience and for that I can never thank him enough.

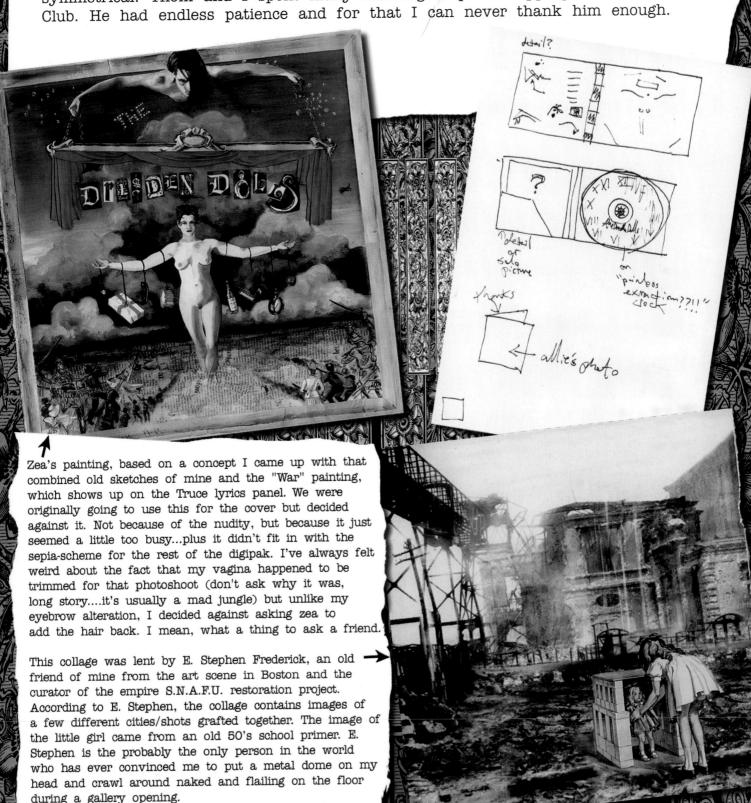

Zea's painting, based on a concept I came up with that combined old sketches of mine and the "War" painting, which shows up on the Truce lyrics panel. We were originally going to use this for the cover but decided against it. Not because of the nudity, but because it just seemed a little too busy...plus it didn't fit in with the sepia-scheme for the rest of the digipak. I've always felt weird about the fact that my vagina happened to be trimmed for that photoshoot (don't ask why it was, long story....it's usually a mad jungle) but unlike my eyebrow alteration, I decided against asking zea to add the hair back. I mean, what a thing to ask a friend.

This collage was lent by E. Stephen Frederick, an old friend of mine from the art scene in Boston and the curator of the empire S.N.A.F.U. restoration project. According to E. Stephen, the collage contains images of a few different cities/shots grafted together. The image of the little girl came from an old 50's school primer. E. Stephen is the probably the only person in the world who has ever convinced me to put a metal dome on my head and crawl around naked and flailing on the floor during a gallery opening.

It must be noted for painful posterity that Zea's painting and E. Stephen's collage are the cover and back of the CD booklet and that they broke up around the time the record was released

31

The booklet insert was my own private undertaking and I
set to work on it soon after the record was finished. My
kitchen became a flurry of papers and glue for two weeks.
I was paralyzed and totally unproductive for the first few
days because I didn't have a coherent concept . . . I just
knew I wanted each panel to contain collage artwork that
was inspired by the song. I was about to go shopping for
cardboard to cut into squares, when I realized that record
albums are the exact same dimensions as a CD. I decided to
use a different LP record album from my collection for the
background of each song and everything after that fell into
place. I used the covers of some and the backs of others.
Unfortunately, if I reveal which records I used, I might get
sued. I tried to cover up as much of the "original"
artwork as possible but still allow enough showing to leave
a scavenger hunt for the obsessive. The first edition of the
CD had much more of the original backgrounds. The second
edition, which was put out by Roadrunner Records after we
signed, has a few key images covered up for copyright
reasons. You can tell which edition of the record you have
by looking at the spine (the original 8 ft releases read "8ft
001" on the CD spine).

The cover painting of the insert booklet was inspired by
Manasse's "War", which I had discovered in a book of
Weimar images called "Voluptuous Panic" (the original
painting is reproduced on the "Truce" lyric page). I
commissioned my dear housemate and painter-friend Zea
Barker (aka "Bony Lil") to create it. She needed some
photographs to work from, so we set up a photo shoot at
Lisa Gordon's studio and brought Pope along to direct it. I
had always had a visual image of things tied to strings and
hanging on arms, so I selected a number of symbolic objects
and tied them to myself with black cord. We also took a lot
of photos of Brian dressed a soldier so that Zea could use
them as reference for every soldier-figure in her painting.

Michael Pope hard at work
with Amanda at album shoot
photo: Lisa Gordon

Brian, Amanda & Pope
getting ready at the shoot
photo: Lisa Gordon

Soldier Brian study for Zea
photo: Lisa Gordon

The original concept was to have Brian appearing as a soldier looking over his shoulder on the side of the painting, but Zea decided that it wasn't going to work with the balance of the composition, so we came up with a second idea: to show Brian in the sky above me, holding onto the marquee which bears the band's name in crumbling lights. Zea set up a shoot in her apartment and took some photos of Brian to work from.

Study of Brian for cover painting
photo: Zea Barker

From the beach shoot with Lisa Gordon. Thom overlayed the border which we stole from an old postcard someone had mailed to me.

The Dresden Dolls

1. Good Day
5:27

2. Girl Anachronism
2:58

3. Missed Me
4:51

4. Half Jack
5:56

5. 672
1:24

6. Coin-Operated Boy
4:46

7. Gravity
4:17

8. Bad Habit
2:59

9. The Perfect Fit
5:44

10. The Jeep Song
4:47

11. Slide
4:30

12. Truce
8:34

I took this photograph at a berlin fleamarket in 1996 during my first trip to germany. I hadn't learned the language yet, I was just visiting with my half-german boyfriend Jason, my first true love. This doll-head was just staring out from a teacup and I thought it perfect, especially since the old man who ran the table at the fleamarket didn't seem particularly dark or twisted, he was just old and grumpy, and I tried to imagine what could have possibly possessed him to think that displaying the doll-head in the teacup like that was good for business, and it must have been around that time I realized I had to spend more time hanging out in germany.

This photo was taken by Riessen during the same shoot that my solo picture was taken. That whole series was from the garden behind my house. I once noticed that both us have our eyes closed in both the front and back photos on the CD.

The Dresden Dolls

8 ft. records

8ft. 001

The CD Release Possibilty Ball...

We planned a CD release party in Boston at the Paradise. About two weeks before the Big Night, we received a call from the printers telling us that something had gone wrong with the printing and that we weren't likely to have the CD shipped in time for the show. We despaired (the show was almost sold out) and wondered what we would do if the night came and we were still CD-less. Thom, who had also designed the poster for the show, kindly made an amendment and tacked this on my door (see tasteful changes in red):

THE DRESDEN DOLLS
RECORD RELEASE POSSIBILITY PREORDER BALL!

AVEC LA MUSIQUE DE
COUNT ZERO
&
WORLD/INFERNO FRIENDSHIP SOCIETY

SEPTEMBRE 26 2003

LA COMEDIE DE
EUGENE MIRMAN

LES OEUVRES DE
EMPIRE S.N.A.F.U. RESTORATION PROJECT

UN SKETCH DE
LES FRERES CORBUSIER

LA MAGIE DE
LE LIVING STATUARY
CREE PAR MICHAEL POPE

ET LE CHEF DE BAND
DAREDEVIL CHICKEN CLUB

AU
PARADISE ROCK CLUB
967 COMMONWEALTH AVENUE, BOSTON
18+ $12 EN AVANCE $15 IL ENTREE

WWW.DRESDENDOLLS.COM

Luckily, the CDs arrived just in time; they were literally delivered to the club itself a few hours before the show. And now, over two years later, here is the completed Sheet Music Companion. As I write these last few words, we've just finished mastering our second record. I am so happy to finally be able to shove these strange-looking notes out into the world, to give a few searching piano players some keys to the doors of these older songs. As I keep learning, nothing ever really goes according to plan. Please take this music and make it your own....play it as you like, how you like, when you like and with whom you like (and god willing, as loud as you like). It's a guidebook, not an instruction manual. Take it and run.

Long Live The Punk Cabaret

Love,
Amanda

Boston
November 24, 2005

September 28, 2003
Just before we hit stage at out
CD release ball at the Paradise
photo: Ron Nordin

Walking off stage at
the CD release ball
photo: Kathleen Doran

About the Sheet Music Itself

   Since I was unable to notate the songs myself, I enlisted the aid of a kind man named Howie Kenty, who came recommended as having done this sort of work for various bands. He began by using his ear and listening to the disc, notating what he could make out. We met only once, and we plugged the Kurzweil straight into his laptop to fill in the blanks. I also wanted this sheet music to more accurately reflect the current state of the song. I improvise these songs every night on stage. There is no concrete, correct music. I didn't want anything to be confused (I assume most people are familiar with these songs through hearing the record, not following us on the road), but I also couldn't bear to think that some of the improvements that I've made since recording wouldn't be reflected in the notes. When things got into listenable shape, Howie sent me mp3 files of the songs (as played by his computer) and I listened and critiqued. After scores of emails, no pun intended, Howie and I hammered out the perfect arrangement for each song.

   Once we had some printable sheet music, I called up my friend Murray Barg, who is the only professional pianist I know in the area. We met circa 2000, when I was taking all sorts of very weird living statue gigs. We were part of a grant-funded project in Boston's main train station that involved me standing stock still dressed as a spring fairy surrounded by two opera singers dressed as flowers. Murray accompanied the singers on a Steinway which was imported into South Station for the occasion. He was dressed as a leaf. At any rate, he was happy to get involved and help me out with proofing the piano parts, and I went over to his house one day to hear how this stuff sounded played by a human being. He also provided invaluable help with the guitar tabs.

Notes for The Player (and Vocalist)

This music is meant to be more of a set of helpful hints than a doctrine. I felt the need to make my own handwritten notes, because typing them in would have been cumbersome and unnatural. The essential thing the player must keep in mind is that the music is changeable. These songs are chord-based, with melodies and discernable hooks and parts, but it is not necessary to play or voice things as they are shown. In fact, you would be playing the music most faithfully if you did not. When I play these songs live, the only thing that generally stays consistent is the bass, and even that can hop from one octave to another. For the more classically-trained, this may seem like an impossible nightmare, but I urge you to experiment. For the sight-reading impaired (like myself) this should be liberating. When I buy books of sheet music, I follow the guitar tabs instead of the piano music, and improvise the rest. This is totally acceptable.

As far as the vocals go, the recordings themselves will probably provide the most insight as to how these songs were intended to be sung. Howie created the most faithful vocal parts he could, but in the worlds of shrieks, grunts and groans, sometimes the type-written word is not enough. I did my best to remedy this problem where I could with my handwritten notes. Once again, these pages provide guidelines and I fully encourage you to change, warp, twist and experiment.

I have made specific Notes for The Player at the end of each song's introduction blurb, which includes helpful tips about voicing, improvisation and so forth. There were several small mistakes in the lyrics which I've chosen to correct by hand.

Decipher My Handwriting (Code Key).....

-I used "RH" and "LH" to indicate right or left hand. Most piano notes are about one hand or the other. In the case of both I usually indicate.

-I have underlined certain vocal words in heavy black. This means Use Force and usually Volume too.

-If I've placed a question mark (?) next to any handwritten lyrics, the choice is yours. I change them up according to mood.

-in a few cases I need to refer to the rhythm and I write "2 and" or sometimes "and of 2" (etc...)

If you notice any glaring errors or have any other helpful feedback, please email sheetmusic@dresdendolls.com
so that those changes might be taken into account
for the next edition.

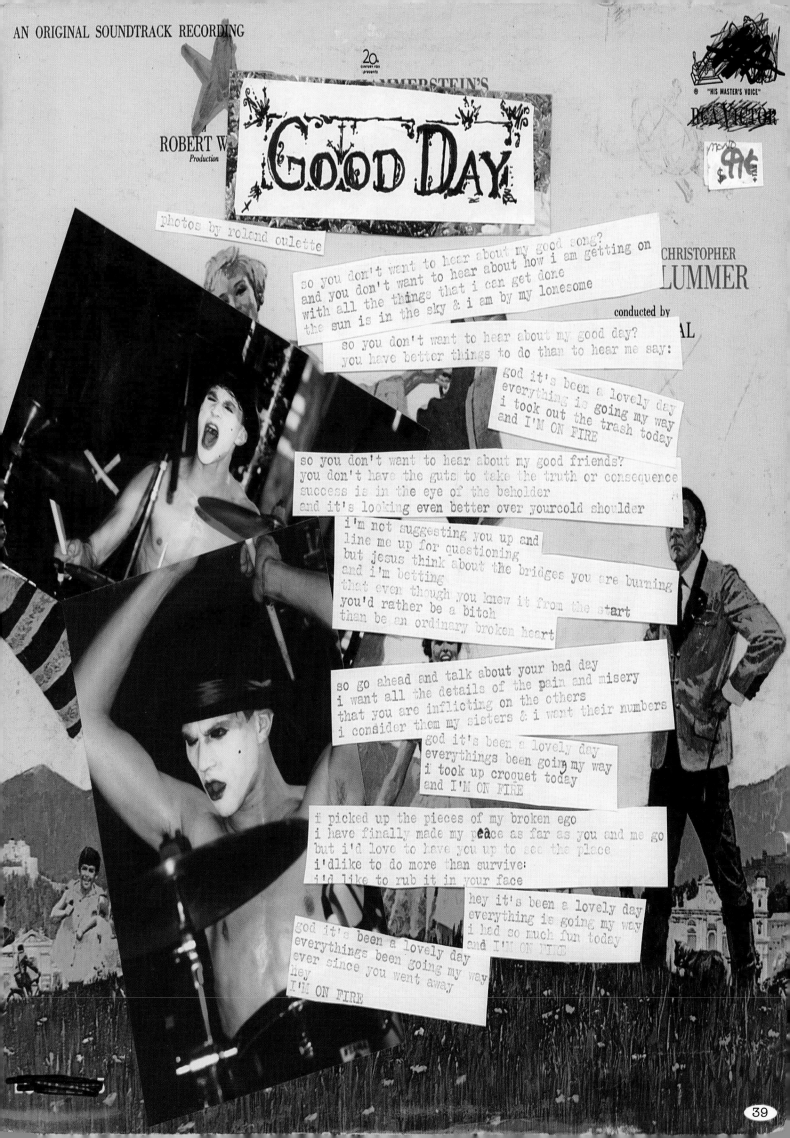

AN ORIGINAL SOUNDTRACK RECORDING

ROBERT W
Production

GOOD DAY

CHRISTOPHER
LUMMER

photos by roland oulette

conducted by

so you don't want to hear about my good song?
and you don't want to hear about how i am getting on
with all the things that i can get done
the sun is in the sky & i am by my lonesome

so you don't want to hear about my good day?
you have better things to do than to hear me say:

god it's been a lovely day
everything is going my way
i took out the trash today
and I'M ON FIRE

so you don't want to hear about my good friends?
you don't have the guts to take the truth or consequence
success is in the eye of the beholder
and it's looking even better over your cold shoulder

i'm not suggesting you up and
line me up for questioning
but jesus think about the bridges you are burning
and i'm betting
that even though you knew it from the start
you'd rather be a bitch
than be an ordinary broken heart

so go ahead and talk about your bad day
i want all the details of the pain and misery
that you are inflicting on the others
i consider them my sisters & i want their numbers

god it's been a lovely day
everythings been going my way
i took up croquet today
and I'M ON FIRE

i picked up the pieces of my broken ego
i have finally made my peace as far as you and me go
but i'd love to have you up to see the place
i'dlike to do more than survive:
i'd like to rub it in your face

hey it's been a lovely day
everything is going my way
i had so much fun today
and I'M ON FIRE

god it's been a lovely day
everythings been going my way
ever since you went away
hey
I'M ON FIRE

39

GOOD DAY

I briefly considered titling this record "Never Date an Actor."

That would have been a terrible title, a wee bit too dramatic. But it was The Actor (or the dramatic loss thereof - believe me, never date an actor) that gave birth to "Good Day," along with "Jeep Song," "Truce," "Boston" (which didn't make the record but is basically "Truce Part I - Before It All Got Terrible") and Colorblind, which also didn't make the record. These all came out in a heap of post breakup venom and sadness a few months into the birth of the band. I was feeling particularly pissed off that The Actor wasn't supportive of my new band (on the contrary, he was jealous of the time I was spending with Brian and with Music).

"So you don't want to hear about my good day?" was the sardonic line that gave birth the melody and as soon as I realized I was writing my own, updated, non-disco version of Gloria Gaynor's "I will survive," I figured I would throw in a little nod to the original (the whole line of "I want to do more than survive . . . " is lifted from that song, including the melody and the bass line -- go listen to the original and laugh). This was one of those songs that practically wrote itself, and while I don't think the lyrics are particularly clever or unique, they were certainly heartfelt at the time. When I need to find motivation to play this song live and mean it, all I need to do is focus my emotion on anyone (including myself) or anything that I feel is belittling or patronizing me or the band at the time. I don't usually have to look very far. Especially as the band grows and I find myself unable to relate my successes to some of my peers because there are those who can be resentful. Morrissey said it best. We Hate it When Our (ex-girl) Friends Become Successful.

I brought this song to Brian as soon as I wrote it and he immediately (as usual) nailed the perfect drum part. It was such an excellent tune for kicking off a set that we started opening with it - it took the place of Half Jack as the usual opening - at nearly every show we played. The guitar part evolved somehow to include Brian starting off strumming the guitar while sitting at the drums, and I gradually take over the chord progression while he sets down the guitar and gets ready to lay into that first bashing drum hit on the first "I'M on fire...." You can hear this on almost all of our live recordings. You can also probably hear some recordings where the guitar is SO out of tune (probably because it's been kicked or moved around) that it immediately stops and the piano comes to the rescue and plays the opening verse solo, sans guitar (there's usually about enough time there to imagine me looking at Brian with an expression that says "what the fuck, is that the guitar?" Brian's expression: "yes, it's out of tune" me: "can you tune it?" Brian: "Shit, I'll try." Me: "uh-oh, that might take too long, we should just start the song, all these people are staring at us." Brian "Okay, fuck it."

Recording this song was actually a lot of fun, because the piano parts aren't difficult to play. We had originally made demo versions of this with Owen at WERS and it was the opening track on our original, humble five-song demo. Brian played the bass on the demo, but for the album recording we recruited our good friend Shawn Setaro, who is not only a great friend of ours but actually the Man Responsible for bringing Brian to the Halloween party at my house where we fatefully met that night in 2000 (we still try to take Shawn out for a nice vegan dinner every year in thanks).

The guitar was another matter. The demo had featured Brian Knoth on Guitar Solo...he was a friend of Owen's who showed up mysteriously at the studio while we were out and laid down what we thought was the most hilarious, out-of-place guitar solo we'd ever heard. The idea that a Dresden Dolls song would even have a Guitar in it, much less a Guitar Solo, made me pee my pants with absurd laughter. So we kept it. Sadly, nobody seemed to think it was as funny as I did. Anyway, when we got around to The Album, we asked my then-boyfriend Ad Frank to please do the guitar honors, and he came down to New York independently of Shawn and fleshed out the song. I wasn't mad about the solo by itself, so when we were doing the piano overdubs I added a piano part to compliment, trying not to step on it but rather trying to create a kind of call-and-answer instrumental.

Some drum trivia: On the demo version, Brian had gone in alone to do drum overdubs with Owen and had hit on the idea of using his keys (and he had a hefty bunch on his keychain) to create that strange sound during the bridge ("I picked up the pieces...") and he re-created that in the studio late one night with Martin while I begged the night off to go into Manhattan to see The Legendary Pink Dots playing at The Village Underground. It was an amazing show, but I missed seeing Brian whip out his key action, which I regret. This was the first song we laid down basic tracks for, because it was so familiar and comfortable for us. Still, I remember the nerve-wracking feeling of sitting outside on martin's fire-escape steps when he told us that we were about to Record For Real. I allowed myself one cigarette and smoked it thinking "This Is It. This Is It. You're about to Record Your First Record. Calm Down. Focus. Don't Fuck Up, or you'll Always Regret It." (Apparently I think in all capitalized words when I'm very stressed out). Then I went down and we nailed the thing in one take.

Notes for the Player:

This song is fairly easy to improvise on and is about as standard as it gets. Live, I vary it all the time and just make sure I outline the chords and give the bass a lot of gusto. It's what I call a "pinkie-killer" because it demands a lot of pinkie action from the left hand (like most songs, the pinky and thumb are used and abused in the left hand, leaving the rest of the fingers fairly ignored). The place that sees the most variation is usually in the bridge, where I play almost completely random patterns over the three-note-chunks that comprise each phrase (you'll see my handwritten notes explaining that). Think that person who doesn't want you to succeed in life, is a fucking bitter twat when you start to talk about your Good Day, and go play.

THE DRESDEN DOLLS

debut album out 9.27.03
SUNDAY 1/25
4pm
All Ages! $10

www.dresdendolls.com

art by Alexandra Mildrag

art by Casey Long

September 5, 2001 Club Siberia
Our first show in the big Apple
photo: Martin Bisi

GIRL ANACHRONISM

you can tell
by the scars on my arms
and the cracks in my hips
and the dents in my car
and the blisters on my lips
that i'm not the carefullest of girls

you can tell
from the glass on the floor
and the strings that are breaking
and i keep on breaking more
and it looks like i am shaking
but it's just the temperature

but then again
if it were any colder i could disengage
if i were any older i would act my age
but i dont think that you'd believe me

it's just the way the operation made me

it's not the way i'm meant to be

and you can tell
from the state of my room
that they let me out too soon
and the pills that i ate
came a couple weeks too late
and i've got some issues to work through
there i go again
pretending to be you
make believing
that i have a soul beneath the suface
trying to convince you
it was accidentally on purpose

i am not so serious
this passion is a plagiarism
i mightjoin your century
but only on a rare occasion
i was taken out before the labor pains set in
and now behold the world's worst accident:
I AM THE GIRL ANACHRONISM

and you can tell
by the red in my eyes
and the bruises on my thighs
and the knots in my hair
and the bathroom full of flies

that i'm not right now at all
there i go again
pretending that i'll fall

don't call the doctors caus
they've seen it all before
they'll say:

"just let her crash and burn she'll learn
the attention just encourages her"

and you can tell from the full-body cast
that you're sorry that you asked
though you did everything you could
like any decent person would
but i lo might be catching so don't touch
you'll start believing you're immune to gravity
and stuff because the bandages will all come off
don't get me wet because the bandages will all come off
because the bandages will all come off

and you can tell
from the smoke at the stake
that the current state is critical

well it is

the little things
for instance:

in the time it takes to break it
she could make up ten excuses
"please excuse her for the day
it's just the way the medication makes her"

i don't necessarily
believe there is a cure for this
so i might join your century
but only as a doubtful guest
i was too precarious
removed as a caesarian
behold the world's worst accident:
THE GIRL ANACHRONISM

43

GIRL ANACHRONISM

Girl Anachronism was started about a year before I met Brian. I was living in Somerville in a Shitty Apartment that I shared with my roommate Monique, and to match it, I bought a really Shitty Upright Piano (which was later converted into Art at my current house) by some guys in a local band who had inherited the beast when they began renting a Shitty Local Practice Space. I paid $300 for it and then paid about $200 to move it into our apartment. After that, I was broke for a while.

In keeping with my old habits, I only wrote when I was alone. Monique had a day job and I was a street performer, which meant I worked mostly weekends and weeknights, so I generally had the run of the place during the day and I would alternate between banging on my Kurzweil in the bedroom and the Shitty Upright, which was in the living room of our apartment (which was Freezing most of the year). This apartment gave birth to a few songs: "Girl Anachronism", "Half Jack" and "Will" (which was the only song we recorded with Martin that didn't make it onto the record).

The idea was simple enough. I wanted to write a song that was a kind of joke-apology to the world for constantly being late, off-kilter, careless and accident-prone . . . the excuse for all my ridiculous behavior being that I was a caesarian yanked from my mother too early. I was therefore Undercooked, Unready For the World, and Worthy of Forgiveness For All of My Shortcomings. The story about coming out early is based in fact. I asked my mum, Kathy, to explain this story in her own words and here's part of the email she sent:

" . . . So now let's jump to 1976. Because Alyson (that's my sister) was a Caesarean birth, our next child was to be a Caesarean birth also. That's the way it was in those days. As they used to say 'Once a Caesarean, always a Caesarean.'

So here we were about one or two weeks before my due date, which was May 3 and I was in the doctor's office. Dr. Altchek, who also delivered Alyson, told me that I would not be delivering on my due date but several days before so that I wouldn't run the risk of going into labor. I had always assumed that I'd have the operation on my due date so this was brand new news to me. He said that the operation would be April 29.

Within 30 seconds he was called out of the room to take a phone call, which lasted no more than five minutes. . . during that time everything came together for me in a rush - - -- I had never really thought about it before, this was the first time -- -- your father was born on a leap year and an even month (but not an even day), I was born on an even month, even day and leap year. Alyson was born on an even month, even day and leap year. And the reason I never thought about it until just then is that I always thought that you were going to be born in May so it never occurred to me that you could be born in April. In those five or 10 minutes I thought, wow, the history of my cousins being born on a leap year, Jack and Alyson and me, wow, now you will be born on an even month. I wonder if I could ask the doctor to postpone the Caesarean one day so then you and Alyson and I would all be even month/day/leap year births? I didn't think he'd say yes but I figured I could always ask. So, remember, Amanda, if it weren't for the phone call that took Doctor Altchek away I never would have had all that time for all of those thoughts to come together in a flash.

When he came back I asked him if I could enter the hospital at the end of the day on April 29 and have the operation on April 30. He looked at me rather strangely but said, 'Well, I will have to go call the hospital and see if the operating room has time on April 30.' He came back after a few minutes and told me that he was able to book the operating room for an 8 AM operation for me on April 30.

When he asked me why I wanted that day, of course I couldn't go into all of the detail that I have just related to you, so all I told him was, 'Well, I like even numbers.'"

Once I started writing this song it split into various sub-plots, which I had anticipated, and were related to feelings of being Out Of Place or Out of Time in general. Everywhere I looked I felt I should have been born to a different era, I should have been born into a different situation, because I certainly don't belong Here . . . Not Now . . . no way. If I could choose? I don't know, I always felt like the twenties or the sixties would have made more sense. Another theme that fit in nicely was a refrain that was given birth to when I was younger: that I was accident-prone not because I was a clumsy kid but because I was desperate for attention. My step-father used the term "accidentally on purpose" for the bruises and cuts and breaks that frequented my little tomboy body, and it made me incredibly self-conscious and confused about what was Real Pain and a Real Accident versus what was self-inflicted and/or subconsciously induced. I was aware of this at a really early age but instead of breeding self-awareness it only created a kind of self-hatred as I bumbled my way through adolescence, convinced that not a single action or movement of mine was authentic or genuine. I felt as if I was a slave to my own attention-getting desires and even the most sacred and real emotions (like grief and sadness and pain and joy) were performed rather than felt. The immediate realization of this often sent me into a vicious cycle or tailspin of crying about something sad, then wondering if I was crying just to get attention, and then again crying about that very prospect . . . ad nauseum.

One lyric that I have a special fondness for is the " . . . but only as a doubtful guest" line. That was added after the fact, while I was dating The Actor, and we used to read and make reference to "The Doubtful Guest" by Edward Gorey, one of our favorite stories. He was this little hairy imp of a specter who hung around a mansion of bourgeois, fur-coat-sporting socialites, wearing converse sneakers and nothing else, saying nothing and being generally annoying, mysterious and out of place. I always related.

When we recorded the demo for Owen at WERS, we recorded call-and-answer vocals for the verse, so that all the lines overlapped. We chose to do a more live feel for the album recording at Martin's, but it was impossible to get everything down in one take since there is practically no space to breathe. When I play this song live, I always have to omit certain lyrics just to find a breathing space, especially during the choruses.

This was the first song we mixed at Martin's, and we were feeling very experimental. I got the strange idea to take out the "3! 4! " right before the drums kick in and put a sample of a screaming baby. We wasted a good hour or two looking for the perfect baby scream from a sound effects CD and we mixed it that way, only to be shocked when we got back to Boston, mix in hand, at how stupid it sounded. So we cut that, thank god.

Notes for the Player:

This song is often played at breakneck speed live, much faster than it is on the album. It depends on the mood. Go crazy. There's lots of room for improv, especially in the verses where it's basically free-form using tri-tones (F# and C . . . the devil's interval!). The intro is also free-form . . . the right hand basically rolls around on that opening chord from bottom to top (C - F# - A - C) until the moment is right and then....

Haldern Festival, Germany
photo:Brian Viglione

"Socks"
art by Lisa Gordon

Art by Sarah Barczyk

October 31, 2002
Identity crisis, schmidentity crisis.
photo;Lisa Gordon

Early May 2002
photo:Lisa Gordon

46

MISSED ME

missed me
missed me
now you gotta kiss me
if you kiss me, mister
i might tell my sister
if i tell her, mister
she might tell my mother
and my mother, mister
she might tell my father
and my father, mister
he won't be too happy
and h ell
and he'll have his lawyer
come up from the city
and arrest you, mister
so i wouldn't miss me
if you get me,mister, see?

missed me
missed me
now you gotta kiss me
if you kiss me, mister
take responsibility
i'm fragile, mister
just like any girl would be
and so misunderstood
(so treat medelicately)

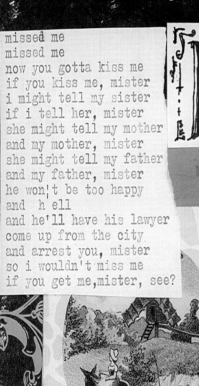

missed me
missed me
now you gotta kiss me
if you miss me, mister
why do you keep leaving
if you trick me, mister
i will make you suffer
and they'll get you, mister
put you in the slammer
and forget you, mister
then you'll miss me, won't you?
won't you miss me?

MISSED ME
MISSED ME
now you've gone and done it
hope you're happy
in the county penitentiary
it serves you right
for kissing little girls
but i'll visit···
if you miss me...

missed me
missed me
now you gotta kiss me
if you kiss me, mister
you must think i'm pretty
if you think so, mister
you must want to fuck me
if you fuck me, mister
it must mean you love me

if you love me mister
you would never leave me i
it's as simple as can be

SAY YOU MISS ME
(how's the food they feed you)
do you
MISS ME?
(will you kiss me through the window?)
DO YOU MISS ME?
MISS ME?
will they ever let you go?
i miss my mister so...

MISSED ME

Missed Me was written shortly before I met Brian, if I remember correctly. The idea sprang to mind as I was wandering around one day with the children's sing-song taunt in my head ("Missed me! Missed me! Now you gotta kiss me!") and I thought about what a wonderful tongue-in-cheek parody it would make. There are only two chords in the song, but it didn't seem to merit any more, just the way most children's songs generally repeat themselves without being self-conscious about it. The piano's melody line is unabashedly stolen (though I didn't realize it at the time - which is typical) from "The Trial" off Pink Floyd's "The Wall"...oddly enough, it's also a sick and twisted song about blame, isolation and imprisonment.

Many people have asked me if this song is about child abuse or rape. The answer is that this song speaks to something which sometimes exists along side those horrible things: a kind of folie-a-deux in which a young girl willingly puts herself in harm's way and then blames an older man for succumbing to her seduction. This is the typical Sexual Confusion of Youth. A teenage girl often wields so much sexual power, but rarely knows how to use it wisely and complications arise. Slide is another song on the record with this same theme . . . the line between perpetrator and victim being blurred

When we recorded this song we decided to use sound effects full-force and Brian implemented all sorts of interesting objects for percussion, including a huge iron gate that happened to be kicking around in Martin's basement. There was a beautiful moment when a car outside honked a horn while I was doing a vocal take (somewhere in the first half of the song, I think) and we decided to leave it instead of trying to edit it out.

It sounded nice and creepy, as did the sound of me shuffling my foot along the concrete floor at the beginning of the track (that's actually me kicking a ricola throat lozenge wrapper out of my way).

Notes For the Player:

The intro can be doubled or even tripled in length, while the right hand improvises. Over the years, Brian and I have made this intro into kind of a game, where I taffy-stretch and then condense the tempo and he tries to guess what I am going to do. The ultimate goal is to hit that final "bonk" together no matter how random the playing in-between has become. I never play this song the same way twice, which is easy because the parameters are so simple. Experimenting with octaves is the key, (try going up to the highest octave possible during the "take responsibility" line, it sounds hilarious) since the notes stay the same but the change in octave can make the song sound even more cartoonish. I also suggest grabbing a friend to play along using pots, forks, pans, bottles and anything else that happens to be lying around.

Grandparents & Small Children Alert:

I've needed to censor this song occasionally for radio or young listeners and I do so by changing the word "fuck" to "touch". It's actually more disturbing.

January 2003: Photo used for
cover of The Noise
photo: Lisa Gordon

Art by Fuser

November 2001
photo: Riessen Kinghorn

HALF JACK

half underwater
i'm half my mother's daughter
a fraction's left up to dispute
the whole collection
half-off the price they're asking
in the halfway house of ill repute

half accidental
half pain
full instrumental
i have a lot to think about
you think they're joking
you have to go provoke him
i guess it's high time you found out

it's half biology
and half corrective surgery gone wrong
you'll notice something funny
if you hang around here for too lon
long agoo
long agao
long ago in some black hole
before they had these pills to take it back

i'm half jill
and half jack

two halves are equal
a cross between two evils
it's not an enviable lot

but if you listen
you'll learn to hear the difference
between the halfs and the half nots

and when i let him in
i feel the stiches getting sicker
i try to wash him out
but like they say
the blood is thicker
i see my mother in my face
but only when i travel
i run as fast as i can run
but jack comes tumbling after

and when i'm brave enough
and find a clever way to kick him out
and i'm so high
not even you and all your love could bring me

down on 83rd he never
found the magic words
to change this fact:

i'm half jill
and half jack

i'm halfway home now
half hoping
for a showdown
'cause i'm not big enough
to house this crowd
it might destroy me
but i'd sacrifice my body
if it meant i'd get the jack part
out

SEE   JACK

HALF JACK

It's very possible that this song was conceived, the ideas developing in my head-womb until one day all the creative atoms and cells came together, and nine months later, give or take, Splosshh, it's a girl! Or a boy. Or a Whatever. It began with my mother hearkening back to a story from when I was a wee bairn.

My parents, Kathy and Jack, divorced when I was just under a year old, and shortly thereafter my mother moved in with my soon-to-be-stepfather John. The story goes that when I was just learning to talk and make sense of the world, I would tell people that I had two daddies. Daddy John, and Daddy Jack. I started musing on this one day, imagining how my little brain must have tried to make sense of this, and how the bizarre, nouveau-parenting network of the modern age boggles the mind. My childhood relationship with Daddy Jack was strange and distant. My older sister and I shuttled monthly from Boston to New York where he lived, but I never felt any strong connection with him....the relationship seemed arbitrary. Why this guy and not some other guy? Did he even care who I was and whether I'd been born or not? Had he even wanted me to be born? Was I a mistake? A happy mistake? A sad one?

To my little brain, it seemed suspicious that my mother took off right after my entrance onto the world stage. I also assumed that my father, like my mother, had both good and bad sides, and the mystery of his personality was that much more ominous because I never intimately knew him the way I knew my mother. It wasn't until I was out of college that I started to realize this inevitable fact: the man is my father and for better or worse, he makes up half of my Biology. It was inescapable. I started to wonder which parts of him had been with me all along. Maybe I had less control over my personality than I thought. These thoughts troubled me profoundly, especially because, back then, I had all but lost contact with Daddy Jack and felt the huge unaddressed question looming over my head: when will I know my father...or will it never matter? I scribbled "Daddy John and Daddy Jack" in my composition notebook, drew a fancy border around it, and decided that there was a song in there somewhere.

I played with the lyrics from time to time, and all sorts of ideas came out . . . too many ideas. I was drinking a lot in those days, and the word-play with "Half John and Half Jack" started to write it's own verses . . . Jack and Coke, drinks made of Half Jack. Half This, Half That. I felt the split in all parts of my personality. The responsible versus the reckless. The kind part versus the mean drunk. The demure girl versus the ranting bitch. Could I pin all the blame on my biology? As I thought more and more, the dichotomy didn't seem to exist so much between my father and stepfather as it did between my father and mother. They were the ones at odds in my head and represented more of a conflict . . . a conflict of loyalty, of sexuality, of trust. "Half Jack and Half Kathy", however, had a terrible rhythm, and I was momentarily stuck. At that moment, the "Jack and Jill" nursery rhyme occurred to me and it all came together. This wasn't just a song about my mother and father, it was a song about confusion in general. Of not knowing what or who I was supposed to be and worse, having no control over my origins and the outside structures that wanted to pitch me into one camp or another. I took the tack away from alcohol and decided to address several themes that seemed to mesh perfectly: my confusing biology (Half Jack and Half Kathy), my confused sexuality (the curse of being a dominant kinda woman with serious penis envy) and the questions I had around my conception and birth. A few other subtle themes leaked in as I drew inspiration from those around me having similar identity issues.

After we did the original demo with song for Owen, I feared my mother hearing it. I had no idea how she would react. But you don't just Not Give Your Mother your band's CD. She didn't take it that terribly. There was one dinner at home where she finally brought it up and told me that the lyrics sort of hurt her feelings (to say nothing of the line in Colorblind: "I love you like a Mother/even after all she's done"). I tried to explain the Hyperbolic Nature of All Songwriting and claimed that everything I write is always a magnified version of some emotion (true, more or less) and I think that put her mind to rest. Not pretty perhaps, but livable.

Jack was another story. I was fucking terrified about how he would react to this song. (I'm slightly terrified of what he - and Kathy - will think of this whole dark-family-history-exposé. I know they'll read this book at some point). Anyway, I was in more frequent contact with him and saw him on the occasional holiday and road trip. I had mailed him a copy of the demo CD and there was one walk, after his mother's funeral, where it came up. I told him not to take it the wrong way, that it was the dark inner workings of my mind and fears, and that our relationship was as good and solid as it appeared. No worries. But the gargantuan task before me was to actually play this song at a concert when Jack was in the audience. This was about as frightening as giving a naked oral book report to your grandparents and current love interests at the same time.

The day eventually came, and we played a club near Washington, DC where Jack was living. I invited him (and my stepmother) to the show. There were about 20 people in the audience. In my Top 10 Regrets of all Time, I rue the fact that the performance wasn't committed to tape. I'll never play that song more faithfully and emotionally than I did that night. I felt every note, every word, every dynamic, with each cell in my body. When it came to playing customized love-and-hate songs for lovers . . . no contest. This one took the cake. I finally understood the heavenly experience I had heard singers and artists talking about all my life. I lost myself in those 5 minutes. I've played it several times with Jack in the audience since then, and every time I feel that creeping vulnerability. But I have to say, it opened a crack, a connection, and I think my relationship with Jack is all the better for it.

The last time we played in Washington, DC at the 9:30 club, he was there. Brian and I sat outside on the balcony after the show, signing autographs, and Jack came up to say hello. He held me in an embrace that lasted over a minute. Everything else melted away, the flashing lights, the waiting fans, the superficial hellos. And in that minute, I felt absolved . . . his embrace, and my ability to allow it, transcended the past, transcended the song and transcended the confusion. Oh, if only every song would do that.

Notes For the Player:

The intro is of indeterminate length. When Brian and I play this song live, the intro is a foundation for a drum solo which can last from anywhere between one and ten minutes. I hold down the bottom D and throw in the above E and then let my fingers wander anywhere they want to go. Lately I've even been switching to A in the bass for a nice shift of key, and then coming back even stronger on the D. Bringing the bass note down an octave (to the lowest D on the piano) is a nice trick. The rhythmic pattern also seems to take on more of an Indian-pow-pow feel the longer we let it go, with an emphasis on the 1 and the and of 2. Other than that, the song is as improvisational as any other... it's important only to hit the bass notes and fill in the upper chords in whichever way you feel fits. Playing with octaves is advised, as is screaming your head off at the end.

August 15, 2002
Sweating in our skivvies in Boston's
dankest dive bar. Mid-summer shows
with no ventilation - a right of passage
photo: Lisa Gordon

November 15, 2002   Bill's Bar
photo: Riessen Kinghorn

See.   Jack.   Run.

Art by Sophie

COIN-OPERATED BOY

This song is not about a dildo. How many times must I explain?

I have a flashbulb memory of the genesis of this song. I was driving towards home down Westland Ave, in the Volvo with the still-broken-on-purpose-radio, and the traffic was crawling. It must have been rush hour. I glanced over at the Coin-Op laundry sign and the song-head started tickling. Coin-Operated Things. Coin-Operated People. Coin-Operated Boy. Would Be Nice To Have. No more of this give-and-take bullshit. Just the fantasy. The rhythm of the phrase itself, so bouncy and march-y, 1...12345, gave birth to the melody instantly and I started coming up with lyrics. I mused in my head until I got home, sat right down at the piano and cranked it out. Everything but the bridge was written, in rough form, within the next couple of days.

It just so happens that I was at the tail end of a frustrating relationship at the time, and was tired of the constant all-night talking and over-analyzing that has gone into most of my pre-breakup eras. As far as I was concerned, I was writing a parody of my soon-to-be-single-again self, searching for the No-Load relationship. This song was a throw-away at best. After I'd lived with the song for a few weeks, I realized that I could save it from the trash bin completely if I added something a little less silly and childish, a meta-narrative so to speak, revealing the actually insecurity behind the joke. So I went back to the drawing board and wrote the bridge. "This bridge was written/to make you feel smittener" was my attempt at self-parody....i was admitting that I was trying to make myself more attractive by being honest enough to admit that my insecurities were a seductive trait that could be used to manipulate. Read that last sentence twice. It's a hall of mirrors, a narcissistic hell.

In pre-production with Martin, I agreed the song could maybe be slightly shorter, so we cut out a verse towards the beginning, which went:

"And If I had a dozen suitors
prettier than you I wouldn't
leave my lifeless lover for a day...
dating's gotten boring, anyway."

Some of our old live recordings house this version of the song....

We had good fun mixing this song, dragging out the sound effects and just getting silly as hell in the studio. The rubber duck remains my favorite. The instrumental section, where you hear the sounds of sawing and clanking, were my idea, and I'm still not sure how well it worked. The concept was to try to conjure of the image of a girl actually building a Coin-Operated Boy....but I think it may have gotten lost in translation.

This was one of the two songs (Gravity was the other) for which Martin pulled out the Memory Man. It was this old-fangled gadget he had purchased for the record, thinking it might come in handy (for you gear-heads, it's an Analogic Echo/Chorus effect box). All those growing whirring effects you hear during the "I want a" section come from the Memory Man, which Martin played and manipulated live onto the track. It was a beautiful thing to watch, knob-twiddling deluxe...Martin on 18 cups of coffee trying to get the perfect squeeky-whirring sound at just the right spot. Back to analog!

As for the skipping and stopping parts, they were developed in rehearsal by accident. I actually fucked up the "go and I'll never be alone" line and we decided that it would be hilarious to not only keep it that way, but repeat it several times. Originally we set the number of repetitions (at 5, I think) but once we started playing the song live over and over again, it was more fun to make the number of skips indeterminate. Brian always leads this part and gives me a cue to end by doing a drum fill that I can (almost) always recognize. The same trick is used in the "I want a I want a I want a" section. Brian and I will play it as long as he feels like it; then he'll give me a drum-fill cue and we'll launch into the "I...WANT....A" breakdown. I follow Brian's hits, and as random as he wants to get, I have to follow him. One of my favorite moments of all time is when a an enthusiastic French journalist was interviewing us after a show in Paris and something to me along the lines of "....Yes!!! Yeees! Zis song eez amazing! For you see, you are controlling zee drummer, like zee pulling of zee strings! And he eez vollowing zee piano, but at zee end....at zee end zis song...YOU ARE ZEE MUPPET!!"

Notes For the Player:

This is an easy and fun song to improvise on, and playing with octaves and voicings is recommended. One of the spot where improv is Essential is the second half of what I call the instrumental. Random notes, random chromatic runs, hitting clusters, the resulting sound should be fair-ground carousel taken over my aliens/mechanical toys gone rabid. The end should be as slowed-down as you wish, recalling a wind-up toy running out of juice (with just a hint of regret).

Grandparents&Small Children Alert/A Note on Ass-Fucking:

Plenty of people have asked me why I chose to clean-up/censor the lyrics on the studio album from "I can even fuck him in the ass" to "I can even take him in the bath". The truth is that the ass-fucking line was improvised at a show long after the recording was made. The first night I sang that alternate line was at TT the Bears in Cambridge, on a recording that ultimately was chosen for inclusion on "A is For Accident" (a compilation of live songs that we released while we were hanging onto the record, trying to get signed). People got so attached to the ass-fucking line that I decided to keep it (unless in the presence of Grandparents/Children /Corporate Radio, where the take him in the bath line comes back to play).

coin-operated boy
video shoot
photo: Lisa Aileen Dragani

Pope & Amanda when we played
with the B-52's at a minor
league baseball stadium
photo: Brian Viglione

art by Lenya Friesner

Pope & Brian
at a friends wedding in NH
we played on a flat-bed truck
photo; Amanda Palmer

photo: Riessen Kinghorn   photo: Roland Oulette

photos from original pressing of "A is For Accident

58

GRAVITY

gravity works slowly & it at all
if you notic e it at all
some of us are getting
mighty lucky
aren't we lucky
if you had to live with this
you'd rather lie than fall
you think i can't fly?
well you just watch me

gravity plays favorites
i know it 'cause i saw
honest to god, officer
it's awful

down at work i'm getting
too familiar with the floor
trading in my talents
by the mouthful

necks are cracking sideways
hit me from the back side
i am on the thin side
you are on the fat side
cut a piece that(s bite size
shoot me from my bad side
if you want a straight line
this'd be a good time

hate to break it to you
but it't out of my control
forces go to work
while we are sleeping

if i could attack with
a more sensible approah
obviously that's what
i'd be doing....right?

now
necks are cracking sideways
hit me from the back side
i am on the white side
you are on the black side
cut a piece that's bite size
shoot me from my good side
if you want a straight line
this'd be a good time

the sky is always falling down on me
so officer,
forgive me
please

GRAVITY

Gravity is what I consider the most cryptic song on the record. How much of a song are you supposed to understand when you write it? I've been wondering about this question for years. I used to write many more stream-of-consciousness lyrics and nowadays I think too much. Then again, I used to have time (or make time?) to sit at the piano for hours and babble, seemingly meaninglessly, into a tape recorder while I pounded out a random piano accompaniment.

One of my songwriting heroes is Robyn Hitchcock; he represents the pinnacle of an artist's ability to write a deep "nonsense" song. There are themes, there is sense, there is meaning, but you'd be goddamned hard-pressed to really explain what it is. My conclusion? If you can feel it without knowing why, it's a good song. I was lucky enough to strike up an e-conversation with Mr. Hitchcock some time ago, and I asked him about this question. He gave me some of the most wonderful songwriting advice I've ever heard:

"...I always think - and sometimes say - that the first person to connect with is yourself. The truer you can be to your own inner compass, the more you will resound with other people; not necessarily everyone, but the ones you do strike will be intensely stricken. Your compass will tell you when you're making true sense and when you're trying too hard. It's a wonderful organ and can be developed over years and years. Good luck with it all."

I had incredibly irritating back and neck and general body pain through my teen years and into my early twenties. I went to an ungodly number of chiropractors, osteopaths, and other back doctors and found no relief and no advice except to "do yoga or some gentle stretching routine." Bullshit, I thought to myself, can't they just FIX ME? Well, the fates played out their cruel hand and now I do yoga three or four times a week and feel just fine. Meanwhile, I spent ten or so years in complete confusion as to why this was happening to ME and what I had done to deserve it. Pinning the blame on gravity (why not?) seemed logical. Fuck this gravity shit. If it would just go away, I'd float around and be happy as a jellyfish. While my 16-year-old contemporaries were fantasizing about boys and girls and cars, I was fantasizing that someone would invent a contraption that would hang me permanently from my feet to relieve the aching, throbbing rack of steel I constantly felt in my lower back.

I was an incessant back-and-neck-and-hip-cracker; I spent a lot of energy in school figuring out the perfect back-cracking technique to use in conjunction with a high-school issued desk chair and I used to ram pencils and ballpoint pens into my neck, causing an interesting cracking sound and resultant blue and black spots which made my neck look like a wild turkey peppered with exploded birdshot. But, I digress, this song isn't really about that. I'm not sure what a lot of the lines are about, but they all stem from the general uncomfortable feeling of living in a suffering human body. I don't know if sharing any of this personal information is at all necessary. Probably not.

At one point I changed the opening line from something I forget now to "honest to god officer . . . " and that gave birth to the additional layer of drunk driving. I imagined a drunk girl being pulled over and blaming this damned gravity phenomenon with her inability to operate her vehicle. When we recorded the vocals for the bridge, I just paced manically around shouting random things while Martin recorded, then we sculpted those four or five takes in the mixing. I used the sonic scene of a drunk-driving accident to inspire a couple of those takes, thus the alphabet, and the idea of a matron nagging a little girl to stand upright (Posture! Posture!).

Notes For the Player:

This is a groovy song. It's best played relaxed and messy, with an emphasis on swinging the bass. I find that the more I move my body while playing, the better the song sounds. The vocally improvised bridge is a complete free-for-all. Just make up some random lyrics. The break at the end (where the bass hand disappears completely) is good for gesticulating wildly in the air with the left hand, or improvising using any G below the right hand.

August 15, 2002 Sweating in Boston's
dankest dive bar
photo: Lisa Gordon

B.R.A. Show December 17, 2001
photo: Lisa Gordon

art by Amalia Gosney

62

BAD HABIT

biting keeps your words at bay
t ending to the sores that stay
happiness is just a gash away
when i open a familiar scar
pain goes shooting like a star
comfort hasn't failed to follow so far

and you might say it's self-indulgent
you might say it's self-destructive
but you see it's more productive
than if i were to be happy

& pens and pen-knives take the blame
crane my neck & scratch my name
but the ugly marks
are worth the momentary gain
when i jab a sharpened object in
choirs of angels seem to sing
hymns of hate in memorandum

and you might say it's self-indulgent
you might say it's self-destructive
but you see it's more productive
than if i were to be healthy

and sappy songs about sex and cheating
bland accounts of two lovers meeting
make me want to give mankind a beating

and as the skin rips off
i cherish the revolting thought
that even if i quit
there's not a chance in hell i'd stop
and anyone can see the signs
mittens in the summertime
thank-you for your pity,
you are too kind
and you might say it's self-destructive
but you see i'd kick the bucket
sixty times before i'd kick the habit

and you might say it's self-inflicted
but you see thats contradictive
why on earth would anyone practice
self-destruction?

and pain opinions are sitcom feeding
they don't know that their minds are teething
makes me want to give mankind a beating...

i've tried bandages and sinking
i've tried gloves and even thinking
i've tried vaseline ...
i've tried everything...

and no-one cares if your back is bleeding
they're concerned with their hair receding
looking back it was all maltreating ...
every thought that occured misleading ...
makes me want to give myself a beating...

BAD HABIT

Bad Habit came out of a desire to express frustration with myself and my inability to stop causing my fingers to bleed. In some sense, it's almost a sister song to Gravity. I was in my freshman year at college and was absolutely miserable. I lived in a cinderblock dorm-room the size of a coffin and had no piano to compose on, just my weighted-key-less Korg M1, which worked in a pinch. It was my first terrible semester of school and I hadn't completely dried-up quite yet (I wrote a total of one other song over the next 4 years).

I remember being really happy with the song as soon as I wrote it and played it incessantly, thus destroying what shreds of possibility there may have been for getting along with the girl in the neighboring coffin, who already hated me. For a few days, I derived special pleasure in playing this song at off-hours just to piss her off. Oh, those were angry times, and I am sorry, Girl Next Door, that I did that to you and also that I krazy-glued together your stupid flip-flops-with-the-zig-zag-in-the-middle-that-when-you-put-them-together-made-a-heart-shape and also sorry that I put disc one of "Einstein on the Beach" on repeat at full blast on my stereo and left for the weekend. Yes, I am. Very, very sorry.

This is actually an easy song to understand and also an easy one to misunderstand. We've gotten plenty of Hate Mail from Angry Parents about this one (go see the Hate Mail section of our website if you don't believe me) and most of the fans who love this song assume that it is about taking a blade to your arm. It's not, exactly. When I wrote it I realized how easy to misinterpret it would be, and I deliberately let the line blur. I do this with a lot of lyrics. Lots of songwriters do. I may never have taken a razor to my wrist or other body part, but I certainly witnessed a lot of that firsthand within my circle of self-destructive friends, and I related the urge to harm oneself with my own compulsion to tear the skin off around my cuticles with my teeth. I couldn't stop. They were getting gross and red and infected and oozing and I was just disgusted with myself. Why was I doing it?

I felt like I had no control over my life, my fingers, my brain, my teeth . . . what the fuck? And who could I possibly ask for help? If I had been cutting my arms, that would've been one thing, but going to the school headshrinker and saying "Help me, put me on meds, I can't stop jabbing pens into the back of my neck and biting my nails!" seemed absurd. I felt completely helpless and screwed-up. So the song turned into an all-purpose hymn for self-destruction in all forms, and how the general self-destructive state of the world seemed to merit a self-destructive reaction. Brian and I had only barely touched on this song, and there was no finished drum part to speak of, since Martin had heard this tune on and old solo demo of mine and suggested we add it to the album. The Amazing Drum Part was born in the studio as Brian and Martin I all gathered round the kit in one of the most musical moments of the recording, as Brian tried things out and we passed feedback between us until he hit on the perfect part. It was a fast, a dirty mix.

Notes For the Player:

This song also has a truly variable tempo. My original solo demo of it is considerably slower than the current tempo, and it sounds great. Play around with it. The verses also have a lot of improv (are we sensing a pattern here? Improv, play around, blurred lines and meanings, etc.) and I usually hit clusters of notes with my right hand at random during the first verse, centered around the ninth (Bb).

July 14, 2002 Axis, Boston
photo: Lisa Gordon

October 31, 2002
Halloween at the Lizard Lounge
photo: Lisa Gordon

die neue zeit
THIS FRIDAY JULY 19

Art by Kelly Fox

The Perfect Fit

i could make a dress
a robe fit for a prince
i could clothe a continent
but i can't sew a stitch

i can paint my face
and stand very very still
it't not very practical
but it still pays the bills

i can't change my name
but i could be your type
i can dance and win at games
like backgammon & life

i used to be the smart one
sharp as a tack
funny that how skipping years ahead
has held me back

i used to be the bright one
top in my class
funny what they give you
when you just learn how to ask

i can write a song
but i can't sing in key
i can play piano
but i never learned to read

i can't trap a mouse
but i can pet a cat
no i'm really serious
i'm really very good at that

i can't fix a car
but i can fix a flat
i could fix alot of things
but i'd rathxar not get into that

i used to be the bright one
smart as a whip
funny how you slip so far
when teachers don't keep track of it

i used to be the tight one
the perfect fit
funny how those compliments
can make you feel so full of it

i can shufflecut and deal
but i can't draw a hand
i can't draw alot of things
i hope you understand

i'm not exceptionally shy
but i've never had a man
who i could look straight in the eye
and tell my secret plans

i can take a vow
and i can wear a ring
and i can make you promises
but they won't mean a thing

can't you just do it for me?
i'll pay you well...
fuck i'll pay you anything
if you could end this

can't you just fix it for me
it's gone berserk
fuck i'll give you anything
if you can make the damn thing work

david wallraf

lisa lunskaya gordon

can't you just fix it for me?
i'll pay you well...
fuck i'll pay you anything...
if you could end this i'll...

WAITING FOR THE SUN

THE PERFECT FIT

There was a time, not long ago, when, for five years, I
made my living as a white-faced street performer called
"The Eight Foot Bride" (the photograph on the lyrics
panel is a one of me as The Eight Foot Bride, in
Bremen, Germany circa 1999). It was an incredible
experience and I wouldn't have had it any other way,
but I began to feel doubts about my role as an artist
and whether I was actually a Productive Member of
Society. I don't know why, but the idea of being a
plumber kept occurring to me. Was I really doing
something useful, or was I just wanking and getting
paid for ripping off the world? I suppose every
performer or artist at one time or another has these
insecurities, and hopefully every one eventually comes to
terms with it and realizes that perhaps there are
plumbers everywhere who live and work in order to
experience Art. It's an interesting question, and probably
merits a book of it's own. Nevertheless, I wrote this
song in the throes of one such self-doubting episode.

I also had lots of rats and mice in my apartment, and
had recently learned how to fix a flat tire. I was
extremely proud of myself.

The Doors quote in there ("Hello, I love You...") came about spontaneously and I asked several lawyer-friends if they thought it was going to be a problem. The general consensus was that it was a short and harmless enough quote to go un-sued, but I still wonder if the day will come when Men in Suits show up at my door, asking me to recall all of our records because we have defamed Jim Morrison. "Hello, I Love You" was one of my first favorite songs to rock out to in grade-school when I'd sit on the carpet in the living room listening to my mother's old vinyl. I loved the fluorescent orange sticker on the cover of "Waiting For the Sun" that proclaimed "Includes the hit HELLO, I LOVE YOU."

Notes For the Player:

This is one of the most straight-forward songs on the record. The only thing improv that's been added over time at the live shows is a quirk during the intro that I've grown fond of: I will play the first repetitive chords (the ones with F# in the bottom) and then skip, out of tempo, to the F chords, à la Good Day, as if the record is skipping. There is no deep artistic reason for this, I just think it sounds cool. If you have a toy piano kicking around, play the high melody line on the toy piano while holding down the bass on the real piano. A toy xylophone or other high-pitched percussion instrument will work. Kazoo is also acceptable.

ich liebe dich.

Memphis, TN 2004
Self Portrait

On the beach at Castle Island near
Boston. first time in the bowler hat
and stripey tights.
photo: Lisa Gordon

Anthony's study, the perfect place to
get your thoughts together.
photo:Anthony Martignetti

art by vince packard

THE JEEP SONG

i've been driving around town
with my head spinning around
everywhere i look i see
your '96 jeep cherokee

you're a bully and a clown
you made me cry and put me down
after all that i've been through
you'd think i'd hate the sight of you

butwith every jeep i see
my broken heart still skips a beat
i guess it's just my stupid luck
that all of boston drives
the same black fucking truck

it could be him
or am i tripping
and i'm crashing into everything
and thinking about
skipping town a while
until these cars go out of style

i try to see it in reverse
it makes the situation
hundreds of times worse
when i wonder if it makes
you want to cry
every time you see
a light blue volvo driving by

so don't tell me if you're
off to see the world
i know you won't get very far
don't tell me if you
get another girl, baby
just tell me if you
get another car

the number of them is insane
every exit's an
ex-boyfriend memory lane
every major street's
a minor heart attack
i see a red jeep
and i want to paint it black

it could be him
or am i tripping
and i'm crashing
into everything
and thinking about
skipping town a while
until these cars

go out of style

it could be him
my heart is pounding
it's just no use
i'm surrounded
but one day
i'll steal your car
and switch the gears
and drive that cherokee
straight off
this trail of tears

THE JEEP SONG

So, now we get back to The Actor. We broke up, and it sucked. What sucked to the extreme was the fact that he drove a car that everybody else in the City of Boston seemed to be driving. Everybody knows this phenomenon, as proved to me by the fact that soon after I wrote the song, someone informed me that across the country, in sunny California, a similar song had been penned by Ima Robot:

They're so popular you can't get away
Girls drive 'em in Encino
And they drive 'em in LA
Some are different, some are older
And their bodystyle is changed
But my heart will still jump
Because to me, they look the same

Ex-girlfriends, black Jettas
Ex-girlfriends, black Jettas
Ex-girlfriends, black Jettas
Ex-girlfriends, black Jettas

-"Black Jettas", by Ima Robot (copyright info?)

Obviously, the Zeitgeist was at work. Check out the heart-jumping line! However, the writer of this song managed to touch on a fact of the Ex's Car Phenomenon that I failed to address in The Jeep Song, namely, the fact that even Newer Model Jeep Cherokees were a pain in my ass, until I saw them from the front and realized that the grille was solid black instead of silver, thus insuring that the car did not house an ex-boyfriend.

The verse melody of this song was also subconsciously ripped off from a song by Sebedoh called "Skull". It took me about a year or longer to realize it, but my embarrassment was minimal. My opinion on that is that there's very little new under the sun and if you happen to subconsciously crib someone else's melody, it's just the way it goes. There are only so many notes and so many melodies to go around. My feelings about this were only confirmed when I ran into Mr. Lou Barlow of Sebedoh himself at the Fuji Rock festival in Japan and he introduced himself to me by saying "Hi, you stole my melody", but continued on to forgive me and to remind me that "Talent Borrows, Genius Steals". Thanks Lou. I will never hear such words from Mick Jagger, whose actual lyrics I crib in the "Paint it Black" line, and I am probably setting myself up for a Rolling Stones lawsuit of epic proportions by actually even admitting that in print. Come and get me, Mick.

This song was great fun to record as we got to drag everybody into the vocal booth for back-up vocals. Ad, Brian and I all took a stab at sounding like the Ronnettes. We tried to get Martin to sing but it wasn't going to happen.

Notes For the Player:

This is another relatively straight-ahead song. I improvise ALL of the right-hand chords, as it's really the chords that matter rather than the inversions.

Dresden Dolls

8ft. records

Summer 2004 The back steps of the house in Lexington, MA where Amanda grew up.

Photo Credit: Scott Irvine

September, 2003
Blake Outside the Paradise
photo: Riessen Kinghorn

art by Jim Brodbeck

August 2001, Playing outside benefit for the Zeitgeist Gallery, before it burned.
photo: Lisa Gordon

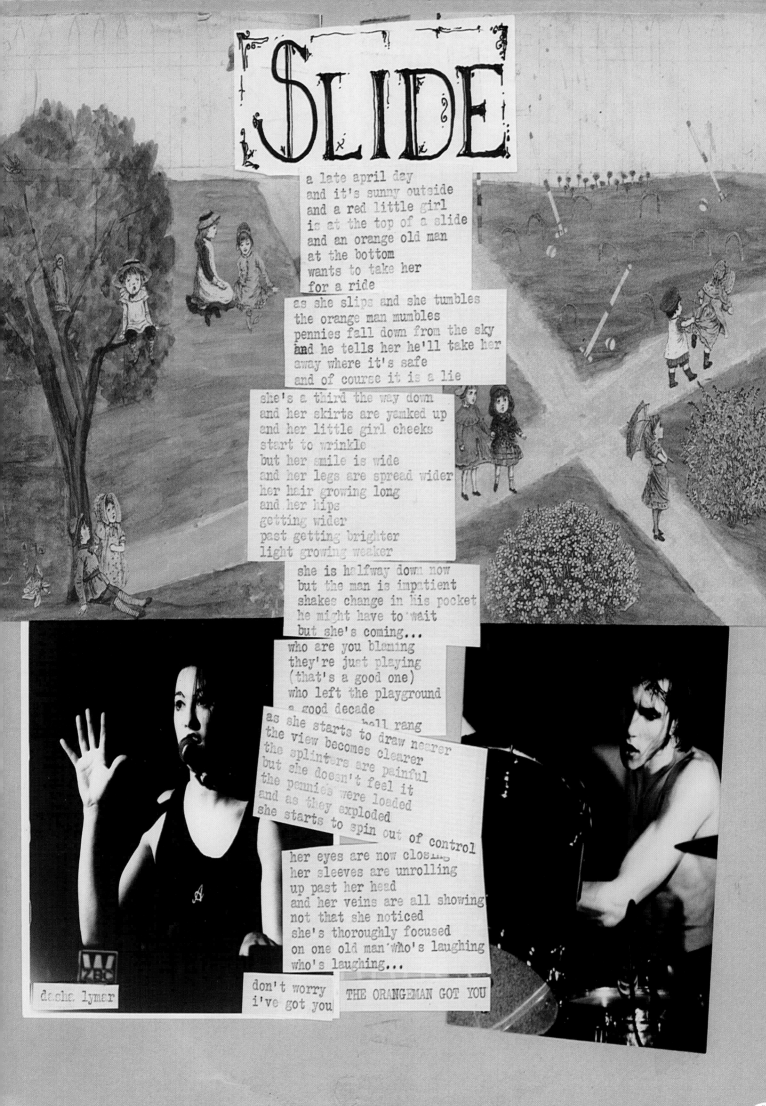

SLIDE

a late april day
and it's sunny outside
and a red little girl
is at the top of a slide
and an orange old man
at the bottom
wants to take her
for a ride

as she slips and she tumbles
the orange man mumbles
pennies fall down from the sky
and he tells her he'll take her
away where it's safe
and of course it is a lie

she's a third the way down
and her skirts are yanked up
and her little girl cheeks
start to wrinkle
but her smile is wide
and her legs are spread wider
her hair growing long
and her hips
getting wider
past getting brighter
light growing weaker

she is halfway down now
but the man is impatient
shakes change in his pocket
he might have to wait
but she's coming...

who are you blaming
they're just playing
(that's a good one)
who left the playground
a good decade
. . . bell rang

as she starts to draw nearer
the view becomes clearer
the splinters are painful
but she doesn't feel it
the pennies were loaded
and as they exploded
she starts to spin out of control

her eyes are now closing
her sleeves are unrolling
up past her head
and her veins are all showing
not that she noticed
she's thoroughly focused
on one old man who's laughing
who's laughing...

dasha lymar

don't worry   THE ORANGEMAN GOT YOU
i've got you

SLIDE

There was a slide at my elementary school, a huge old-fashioned metal one with at least 15 or 20 steps. This was the Slide that always comes to mind when I think about this song. It's strange, these slides don't seem to exist anymore; we had talked about doing a video for this song and when we tried to find one, we learned they were impossible to locate. Every one of them had been torn down and replaced by safer, friendlier and more colorful playground furniture made out of plastic and rubber. I can't stand it.

Notes For the Player:

This one is pretty straight ahead. I often improvise the right-hand melody during the instumental bits in the middle of the song, and the crashing bridge can be fudged to sound a little more out of control, with more experimental notes around the written chords.

July 14, 2002 Axis, Boston
photo: Dasha Lymar

"A Third The Way Down"
pastel by Barnaby Whitfield

April 14, 2004
photo:Ron Nordine

July 2004
photo: Lisa Aileen Dragani

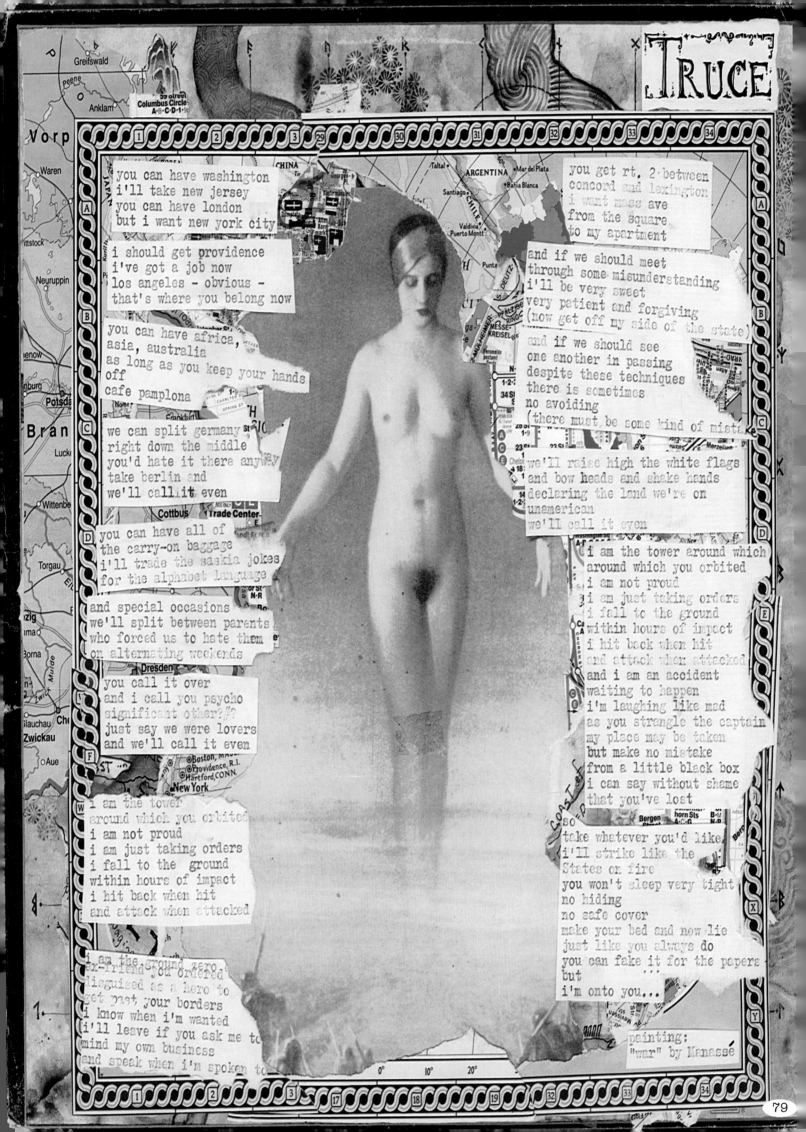

TRUCE

you can have washington
i'll take new jersey
you can have london
but i want new york city

i should get providence
i've got a job now
los angeles - obvious -
that's where you belong now

you can have africa,
asia, australia
as long as you keep your hands
off
cafe pamplona

we can split germany
right down the middle
you'd hate it there anyway
take berlin and
we'll call it even

you can have all of
the carry-on baggage
i'll trade the saskia jokes
for the alphabet language

and special occasions
we'll split between parents
who forced us to hate them
on alternating weekends

you call it over
and i call you psycho
significant other?"?
just say we were lovers
and we'll call it even

i am the tower
around which you orbited
i am not proud
i am just taking orders
i fall to the ground
within hours of impact
i hit back when hit
and attack when attacked

i am the ground zero
ex-friend you ordered
disguised as a hero to
get past your borders
i know when i'm wanted
i'll leave if you ask me to
mind my own business
and speak when i'm spoken to

you get rt. 2 between
concord and lexington
i want mass ave
from the square
to my apartment

and if we should meet
through some misunderstanding
i'll be very sweet
very patient and forgiving
(now get off my side of the state)

and if we should see
one another in passing
despite these techniques
there is sometimes
no avoiding
(there must be some kind of mistake

we'll raise high the white flags
and bow heads and shake hands
declaring the land we're on
unamerican
we'll call it even

i am the tower around which
around which you orbited
i am not proud
i am just taking orders
i fall to the ground
within hours of impact
i hit back when hit
and attack when attacked
and i am an accident
waiting to happen
i'm laughing like mad
as you strangle the captain
my place may be taken
but make no mistake
from a little black box
i can say without shame
that you've lost

so
take whatever you'd like
i'll strike like the
States on fire
you won't sleep very tight
no hiding
no safe cover
make your bed and now lie
just like you always do
you can fake it for the papers
but
i'm onto you...

painting:
"war" by Manassé

79

TRUCE

Some time around the actor-breakup, jeep-avoiding era in the summer of 2001, I was traveling along Storrow Drive in the Volvo and started thinking about the divvying up of certain places and friends that must inevitable take place when two people part ways bitterly. I was dreading walking through familiar, beloved places and having the specter of "oh no he may be there or I may run into his friends" haunting me wherever I went. How convenient it would be if we could have just met on common ground and divided the city up as in a divorce settlement. And why stop at the city? Take precaution. Divide up the world to prevent any possible conflicts, like generals negotiating in the war room. Soon after these thoughts occurred and I wrote the first few verses but hadn't gotten much farther, he moved to New York. I felt a huge relief but also a sadness at the possibility that The Actor felt he needed to leave a city just to be free of all traces of our relationship. We didn't phone, we didn't write, he refused to have anything to do with me. I mourned the death of a possible friendship, and hoped things would change. A few weeks later, the World Trade Center got struck by two airplanes and collapsed. I knew he was there in the city, somewhere, and the rest of the lyrics came crashing down like so much office paper and debris. The profound smallness of our petty relationship in the face of this man-made catastrophe was glaring.

Recording and mixing this song was a mother because we decided to bring in a small string section in the form of Jonah Sacks, my cello-laying ex-boyfriend (that break-up was, happily, an amicable one) and Sasha Forte, our friend from King Missile, on viola. We sent them recordings of our demo and asked them to get familiar with the outro, then we just sat around a arranged on the spot, with a lot of input from Martin, when they came in. We left the musicians out of the mixing process, but since none of us were experts in String Arranging, there were plenty or arguments during the mixing. I think it's the one time anyone actually stormed out of a session altogether. It took hours upon hours to mix, but we ended up satisfied.

Notes For the Player:

This is one of my absolute favorite songs to play live, because it's so flexible. This song has patterns that can fit any number of notes, and I always play with the variations. The lilting rhythm is key, the notes can expand and contact as you wish. Sometimes adding the more middle-eastern sounding runs (throwing in the ? find key....) will work. The intro is completely open and can be repeated infinite times. When my voice is weak during a set, I'll sometimes stretch this intro into a good two or three minutes to give it a rest. Improvising over the basics bass notes (D and C) is lots of fun when you try to quote little snippets of the outro (i.e. the melodies that center around the C-diminished chord).

Also notable is the ending rock section ("take whatever you like...."), which we realized I had unwittingly stolen from Fugazi's "Blueprint". We ran with that one, and just added Blueprint to the set after Truce, almost melding them together. When we went into the studio, we deliberately changed part of that section (throwing in the Eb and Gb over the main D chord when improvising during the instrumentals) to prevent it from sounding like a direct rip-off. The change never stuck and we always use the original chord when we play the song live, but in retrospect I think the alternate album chord sounds kind of cool. In any even, we chose to notate it the live way, so you will notice a discrepancy with the album.

The instrumental at the end is a monster, and should be played with total abandon and improv. Just following in the bass notes and banging out one single chord repeatedly (C-Eb-A) would work. It's more about force and dynamic than melody, but both should be represented. Coming up with new runs and melodies for this section is a game I play with myself when we toured with the song a lot. Like the intro, the outro can be extended longer if you so desire....Brian and I tend to do that if things are going particularly well or we felt we haven't quite come to end by the time the fourth repetition rolls around.

Summer 2002
photo: Kelly Davidson

Summer 2004 Berlin, Germany
Self Portrait

November 1, 2000
Brian exploring Amanda's
apartment the first time
photo: Amanda Palmer

art by Bayla Laks

The DRESDEN DOLLS

the

DON'T LET THE BROKEN DOLLY SUFFER .. *Get Her a New Wig or Head*

www.dresdendolls.com

additional musicians:
martin bisi - memoryman on6, 7 &9
sasha forte - violin & viola on 12
ad frank - elec. guitar on 1
         & back-up vocals on 10
shawn setaro - bass on 1, 7 & 10
         &acoustic guitar on 7
jonah sacks - cello on 12
brian also plays acoustic guitar
& sings back-up on 10
string arrangement on 12 by
    jonah, sasha, martin & the dolls

album design by amanda palmer &
booklet collages by amanda palmer

cover&graphic layout by thomas martin

design help from steve martin

album cover photo by lisa lunskya gordon

ad frank appears courtesy
of stop, pop & roll records

rubble dollhouse image courtesy of
the empire s.n.a.f.u. restoration project
(www.empiresnafu.org)

booklet cover painting by zea barker

THE DRESDEN DOLLS are:

amanda palmer -
piano, toy piano & vocals

brian viglione -
drums & percussion

produced by martin bisi & the dresden dolls

all songs written and composed
by amanda palmer (ASCAP)

engineered by martin bisi at b.c. studio, brooklyn ny
mastered by fred kevorkian at absolute audio, ny ny

16
Great Songs

all songs ©℗ 2003 amanda palmer

all photos of the dolls by
riessen kinghorn unless noted
otherwise; main portrait of
brian by melissa mahoney

the dresden dolls thank:
andrew anselmo (love to the engine room), zea barker, lee barron,
rick berlin, aria boutet, joshua boyle, noah blumenson-cooke,
owen curtin, veronique d'entrement, nathan elbogen, ad frank,
d. franklin, e. stephen frederick, gus & toscanini's, john s.
hall & king missile, important john&jill, joshua knobe, michael
knoblach, kumalisa, pan 9, michael pope, emily maiden, anthony
martignetti, the martin brothers (steve&thom); luq mcdermot,
the west coast mockett family, mutti & johann, the radical
artist foundation, ron nordin, helena prezio, bradford reed,
laura sanford, steve&don at copytech, alina simone, sean slade,
the throes nyc, nick vargelis, ma viglione, pa viglione, maia
viglione, matt wood, matvei yankelevich, meredith yayanos,
the zeitgeist gallery & too many others to name

photo behind disc
by alina simone

dolls on couch photo
by kelly davidson

dollhead photo by
amanda palmer
berlin flohmarkt 1993

"accept the worst, expect the worst, DEMAND the worst"
-karen mantler

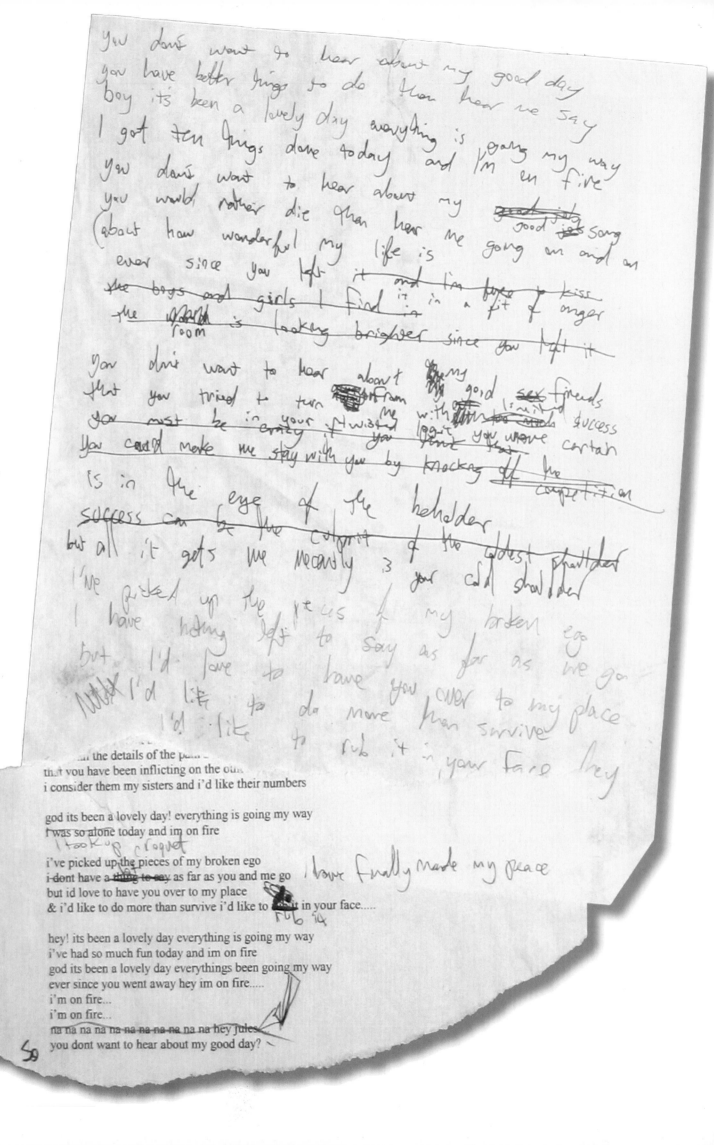

you dont want to hear about my good day
you have better things to do than hear me say
boy its been a lovely day everything is going my way
I got ten things done today and I'm on fire
you dont want to hear about my ~~good job~~ song
you would rather die than hear me going on and on
(about how wonderful my life is
ever since you left it ~~and I'm dying to kiss~~
~~the boys and~~ girls I find ~~it in a fit of anger~~
~~the world~~ is looking brighter since you left it
room

you dont want to hear about ~~my~~ good ~~sex~~ friends
~~that you tried to turn~~ ~~from me with~~ limited success
~~you must be in your~~ twisted logic ~~if you~~ ~~you were~~ certain
~~you could make me stay with you by knocking off the competition~~
is in the eye of the beholder
~~success can be the culprit of the coldest shoulder~~
but all it gets me nearly s your cold shoulder
I've picked up the pieces of my broken ego
I have ~~nothing left~~ to say as far as we go
but I'd love to have you over to my place
I'd like to do more than survive
I'd like to rub it in your face hey

the details of the pain
that you have been inflicting on the ou
i consider them my sisters and i'd like their numbers

god its been a lovely day! everything is going my way
i was so alone today and im on fire
I took up croquet
i've picked up the pieces of my broken ego
i dont have a ~~thing to say~~ as far as you and me go   I have finally made my peace
but id love to have you over to my place
& i'd like to do more than survive i'd like to ~~shout~~ in your face.....
rub it
hey! its been a lovely day everything is going my way
i've had so much fun today and im on fire
god its been a lovely day everythings been going my way
ever since you went away hey im on fire.....
i'm on fire...
i'm on fire...
na na na na na na na na na na na hey jules
you dont want to hear about my good day? ~

Music and Lyrics by
Amanda Palmer

85

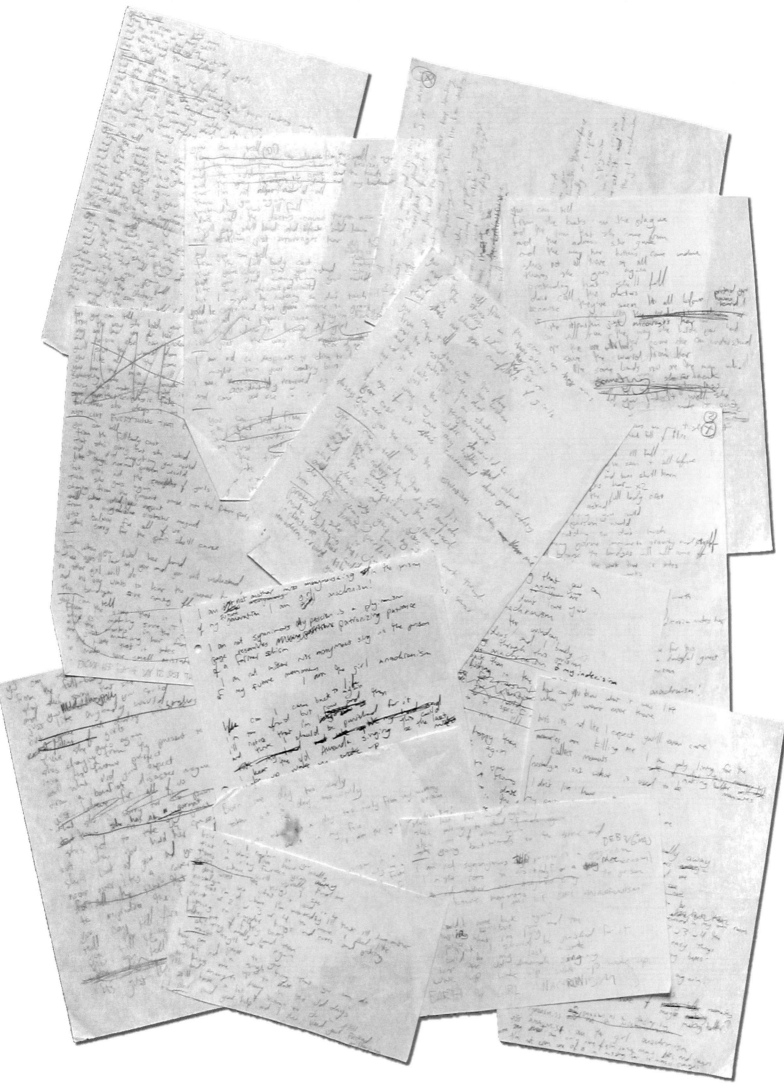

GIRL ANACHRONISM

Music and Lyrics by
Amanda Palmer

tend-ing to be you,___ Make-be-liev-ing that I have a soul be-neath the sur-face, try-ing to con-vince you it was

ac-ci-dent-al-ly on pur-pose.

Frenetic... yaaaaa

I am not so se-ri-ous, this pas-sion is a pla-gia-ri-sm. I might join your cen-tu-ry but on-ly on a rare oc-ca-sion.

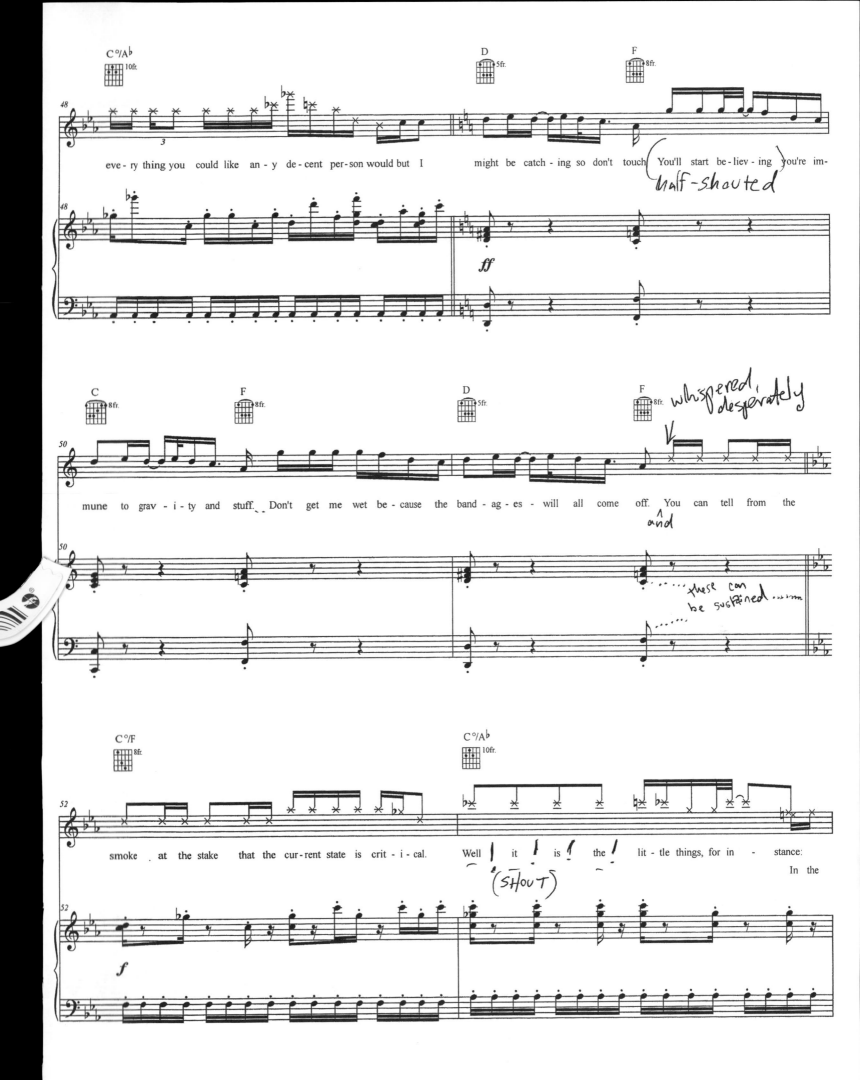

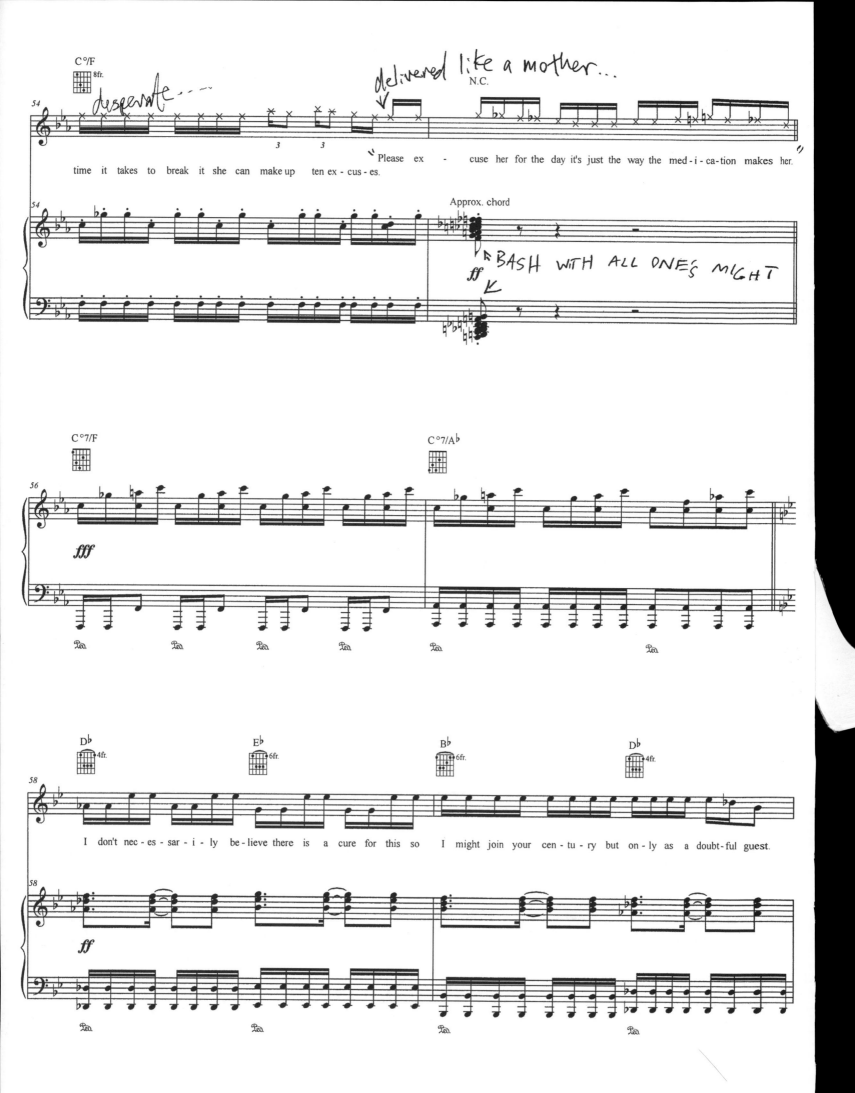

Music and Lyrics by
Amanda Palmer

107

108

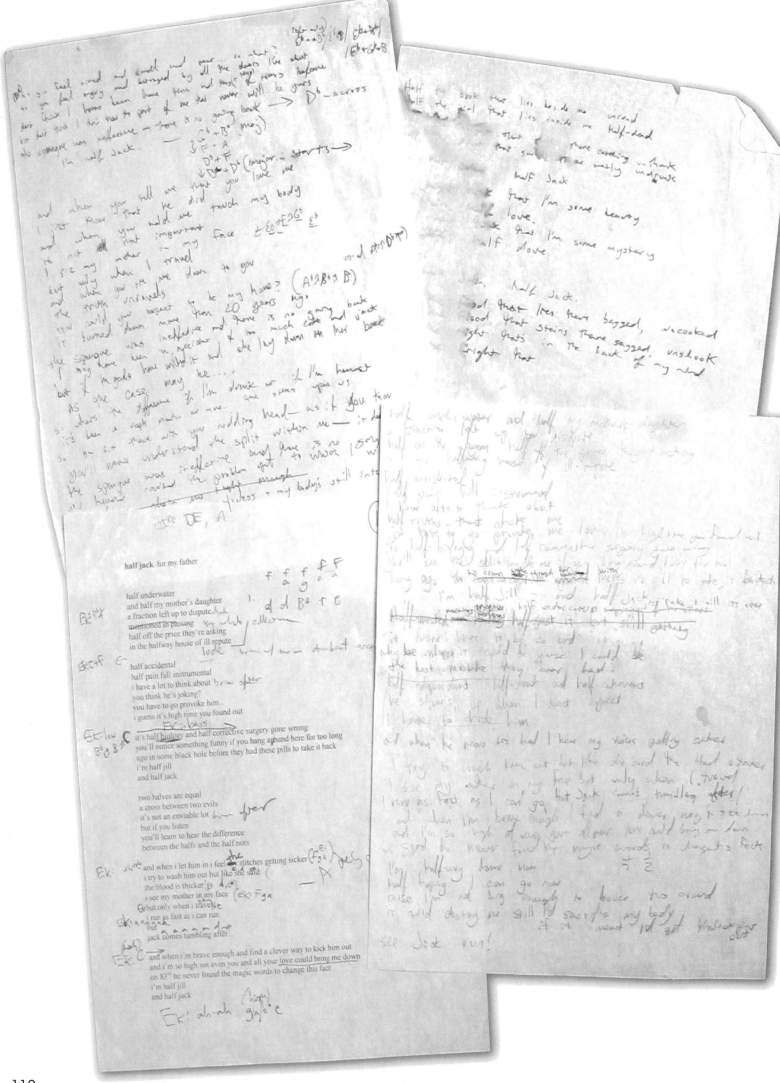

half jack for my father

half underwater
and half my mother's daughter
a fraction left up to dispute
mentioned in passing
half off the price they're asking
in the halfway house of ill repute

half accidental
half pain full instrumental
i have a lot to think about
you think he's joking?
you have to go provoke him.
i guess it's high time you found out

it's half biology and half corrective surgery gone wrong
you'll notice something funny if you hang around here for too long
ago in some black hole before they had these pills to take it back
i'm half jill
and half jack.

two halves are equal
a cross between two evils
it's not an enviable lot
but if you listen
you'll learn to hear the difference
between the halfs and the half nots

and when i let him in i feel the stitches getting sicker
i try to wash him out but like she said
the blood is thicker
i see my mother in my face
but only when i travel
i run as fast as i can run
jack comes tumbling after

and when i'm brave enough and find a clever way to kick him out
and i'm so high not even you and all your love could bring me down
on 83rd he never found the magic words to change this fact
i'm half jill
and half jack

Music and Lyrics by
Amanda Palmer

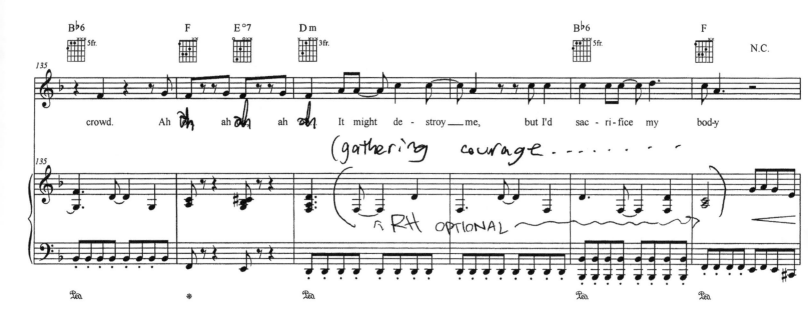

coin operated boy Ⓖ
he can play it shy mechanical and coy
but I know he feels like a boy should feel
isn't that the point isn't that what's real
uh uh uh
coin operated boy
  set up in the store he is just a toy
but I turn him on and he comes to life
isn't ~~that~~ ~~the~~ ~~point~~ that is why I want my
      he   a joy
      be
coin operated boy

Ⓐ made of plastic and elastic
  he is ~~~~ and long-lasting
        rugged
who could ever ever ask for more
other boys are dirty and a bore
with a life-time guarantee
included with his batteries
i'll never need to cry at night again
~~~~ keep feeding him quarters and pretend...
            him

coin-operated boy
~~you can change the sound of his pretty voice~~
with his ~~pretty~~ coin-operated voice
saying that he loves me ~~that~~ he's thinking of me ...
~~it could say things say things to me all day~~
                                    he will stay with me forever more
uh uh uh   ~~and~~ ~~mother~~ ~~says~~..o boy I need another
coin-operated boy
he can play it shy mechanical and coy
but I know he feels like a boy should feel
isn't that the point, isn't that what's real)

121

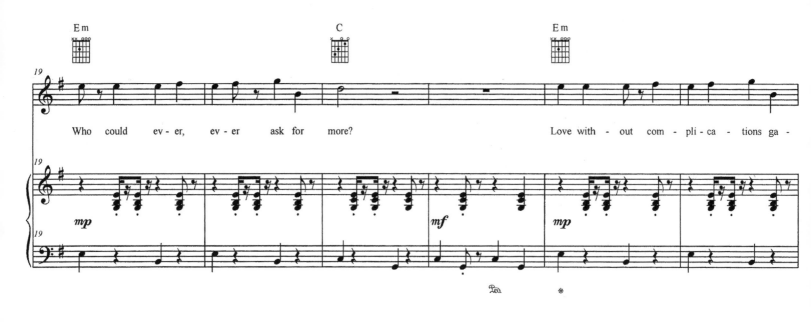

Who could ev-er, ev-er ask for more? Love with-out com-pli-ca-tions ga-

lore... Man-y shapes and weights to choose from, I will nev-er leave my bed-room.

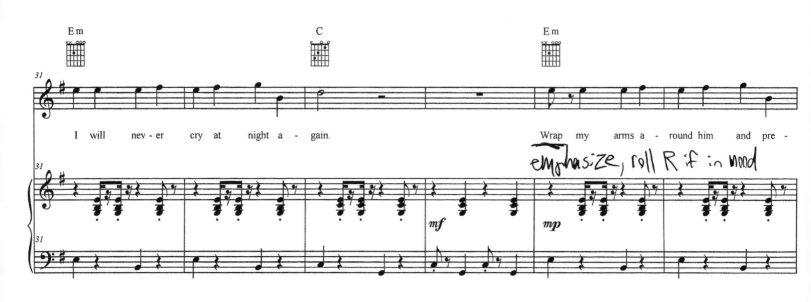

I will nev-er cry at night a-gain. Wrap my arms a-round him and pre-

emphasize, roll R if in mood

127

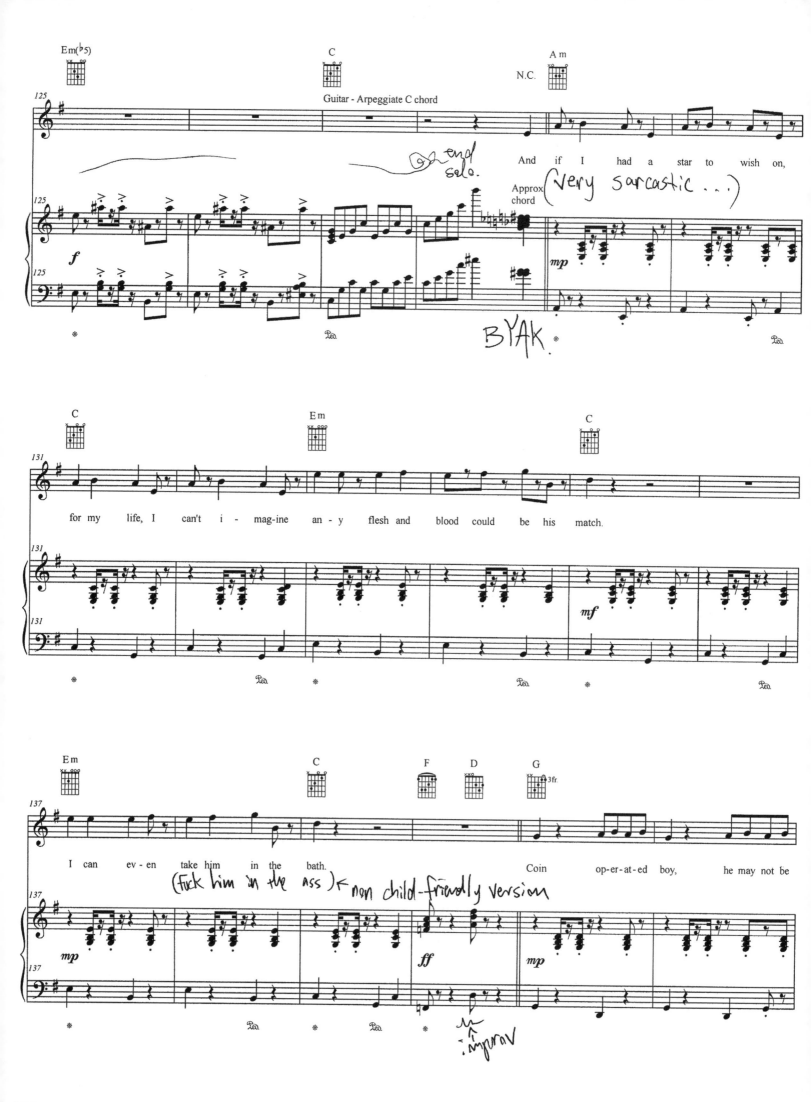

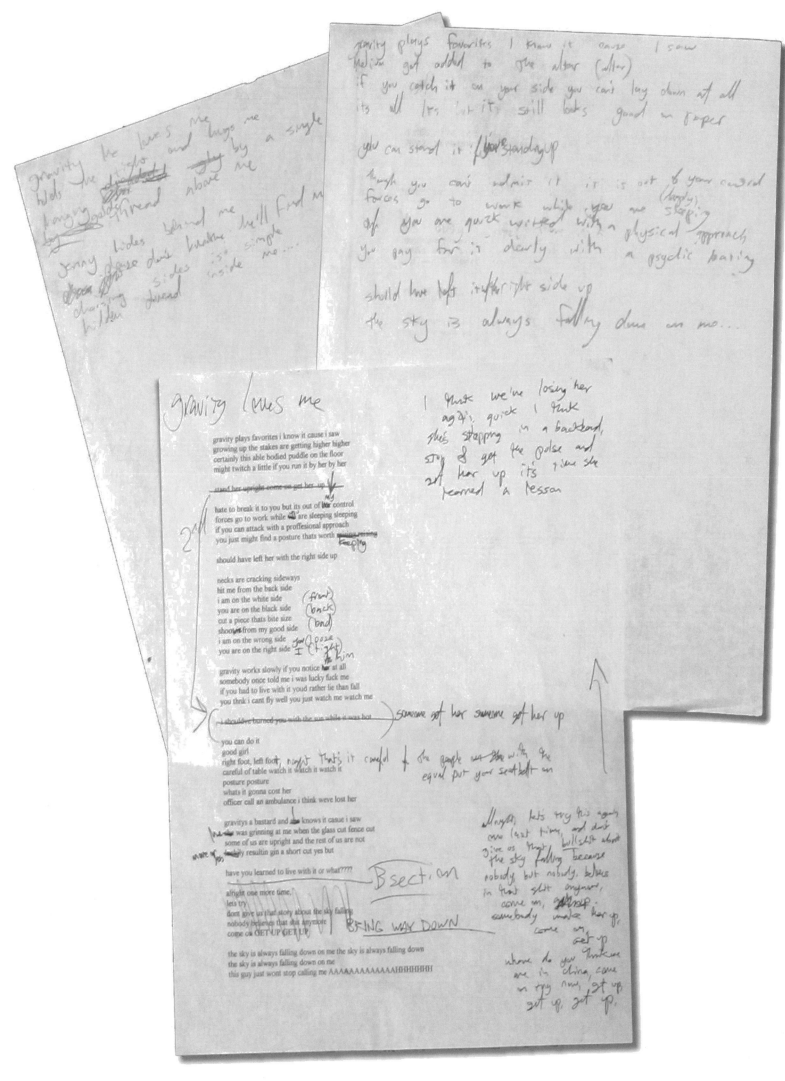

130

GRAVITY

Music and Lyrics by
Amanda Palmer

BLUESY & SEXY

Guitar - Follow bassline between playing chords.

131

flail wildly with left hand
for stunning visual effect.

Music and Lyrics by
Amanda Palmer

choirs of an- gels seem to sing hymns of hate __ in mem-o- ran - dum. _____ And

you might say it's self in-dul- gent, you might say it's self - de-struc- tive, but, you see, it's more pro-duc- tive

than if I __ were to be _____ hap- py... _____ And sap-py songs a-bout sex and cheat-ing,

Fm   Ab   Fm   Ab(add#11)

bland ac-counts of two lov-ers___ meet-ing   make me want to give man-kind a   beat - ing.___

classic jackhammer bass part!

EbM7   Ab(add#11)   EbM11   Eb   EbM11   Eb

                                                                                        And

Cm   Eb   Cm   Eb   Cm

you might say it's self - de-struc - tive, but, you see, I'd kick the buck-et six-ty times___ be-fore I'd kick the___

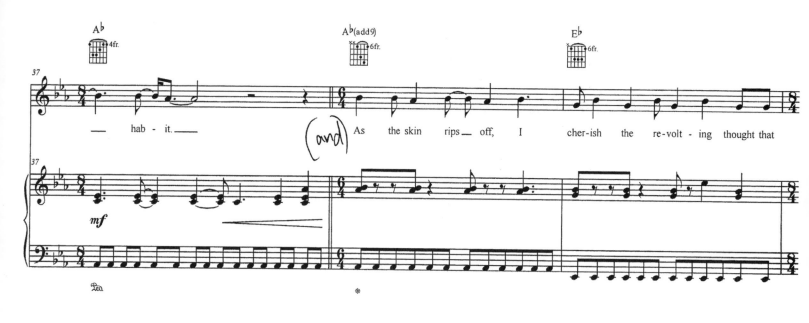

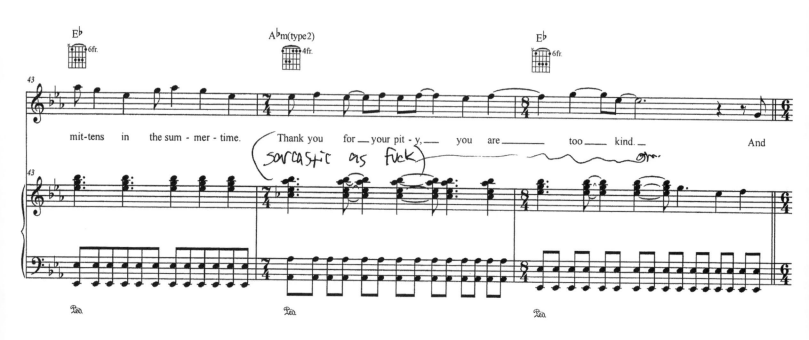

142

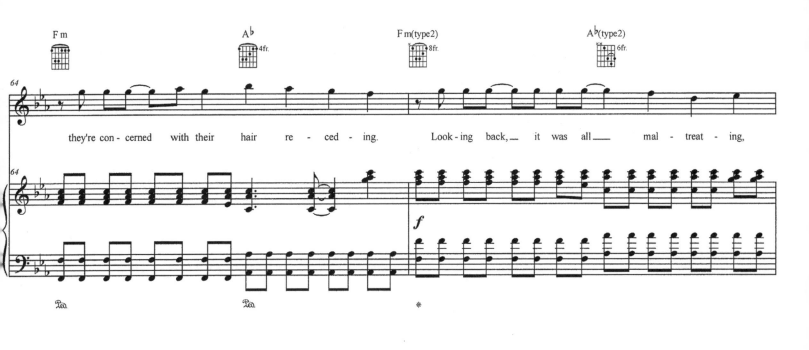

they're con - cerned with their hair re - ced - ing. Look - ing back,___ it was all___ mal - treat - ing,

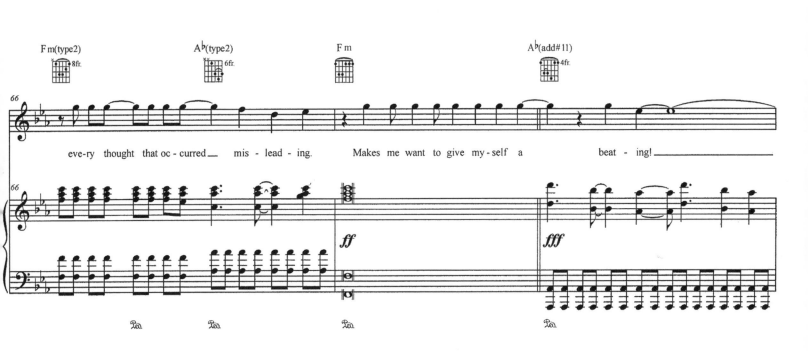

eve - ry thought that oc - curred___ mis - lead - ing. Makes me want to give my - self a beat - ing!___

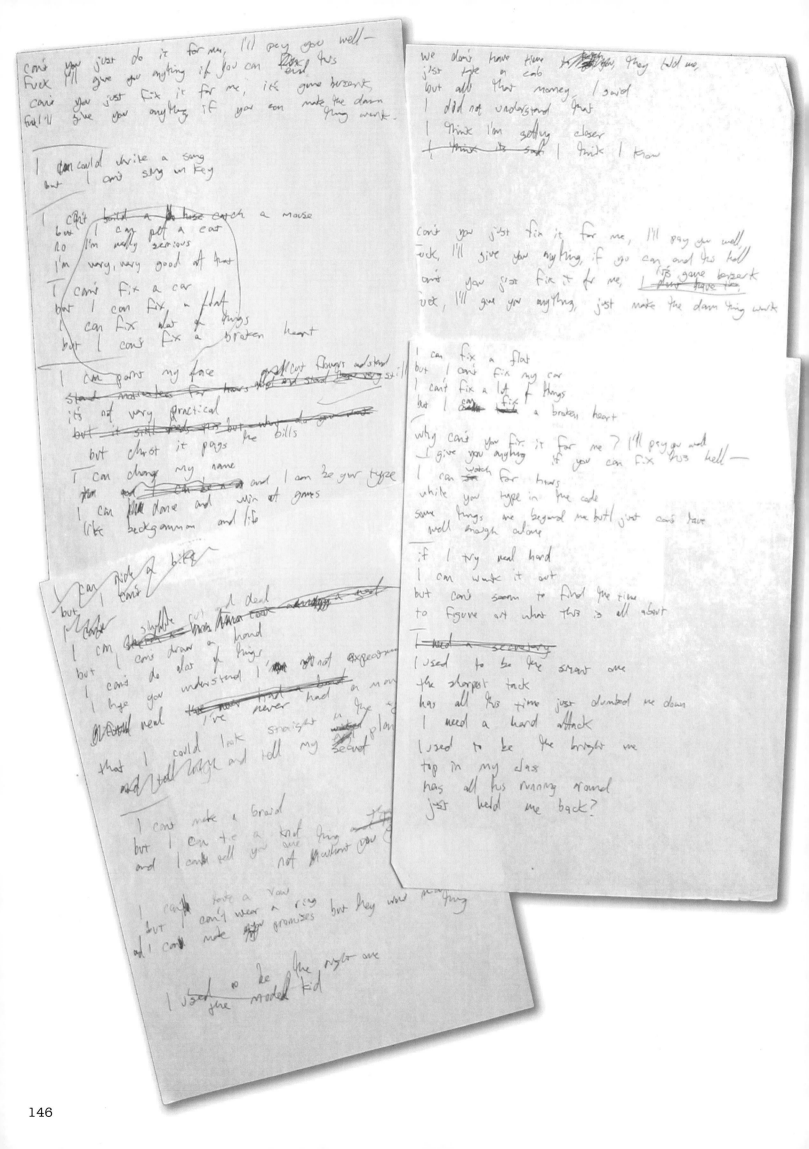

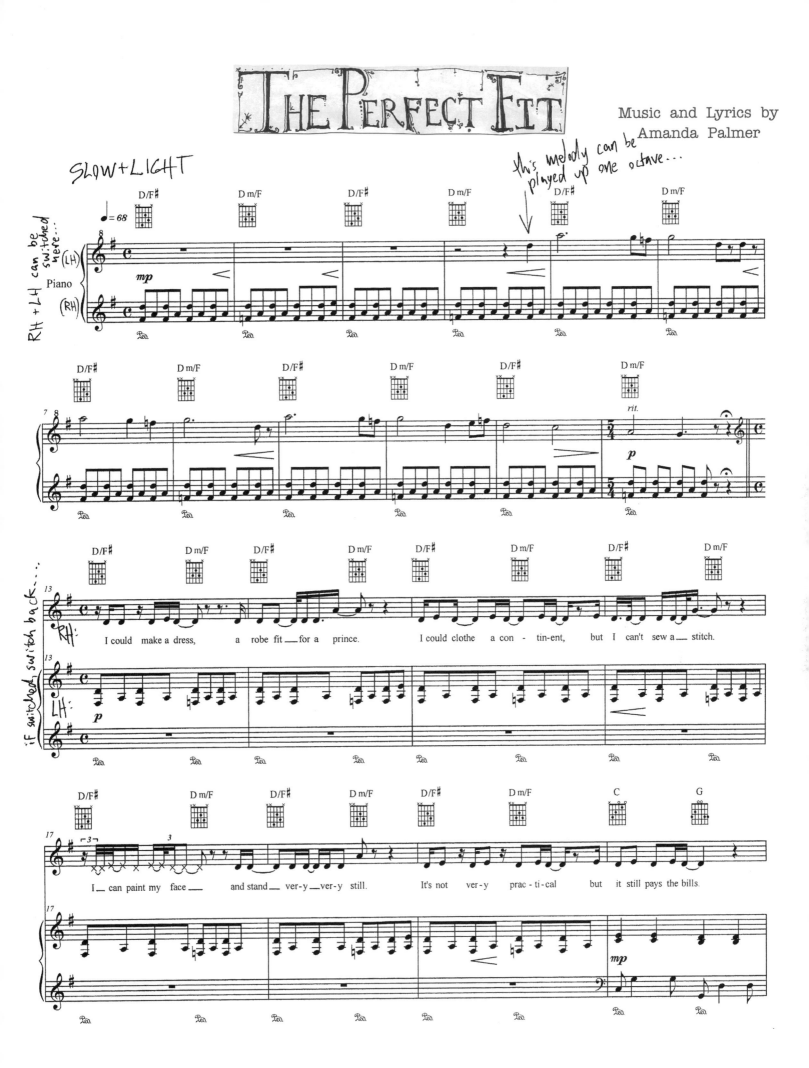

147

I used to be __ the bright one, smart as a __ whip. Fun-ny how you slip so far when teach-ers don't keep track of it.

I used to be __ the tight one, the per-fect fit. __ Fun-ny how those com-pli-ments can make you feel so __ full of it.

RH can improvise/solo here.....

I can

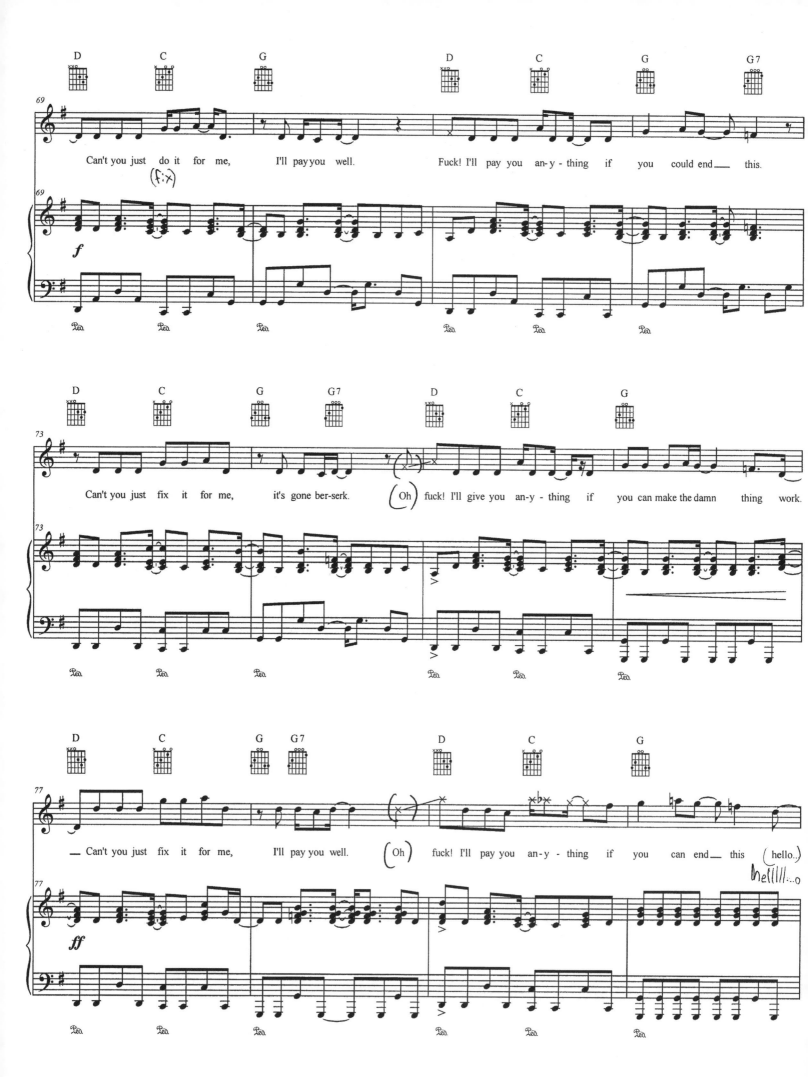

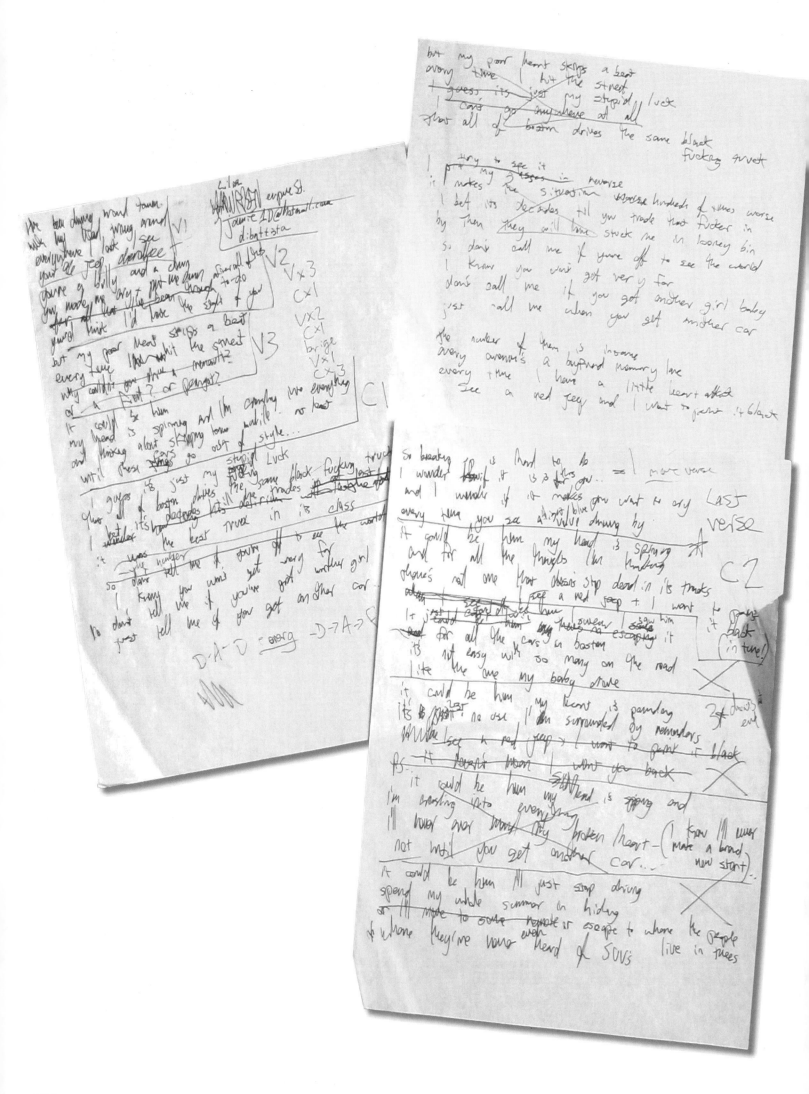

Music and Lyrics by
Amanda Palmer

UPBEAT & GIRL-GROUP LIKE

Guitar - Arpeggiate chords

I've been driv-ing a - round town with my head spin-ning a - round. Eve-ry - where I look I see your nine-ty six Jeep Cher-o - kee. You're a bul -

155

162

and drive that Cher-o-kee___ straight off this trail of

tears.

(Ba - da - da - ba - ba - ba - da - da - da - da - Ba - ba - da - da - ba - ba - ba - da - da - da - da -

Ba - ba - ba - da - ba - ba - ba - da - da - da - da - Ba - ba - ba - da - ba - ba - ba - da - da - da - da - da...)___

SING IT....

end can be held & jangled around for effect.

163

her sleeves are unrolling, up past
her head and flew into the sandbox
not that she noticed her senses
were focused on one old man who's
laughing...
don't worry... I've got you
THE ORANGEMAN GOT YOU

what is passed (past)
manichild dreams in a puddle of light
and a red little girl's at the top of a slide
and an orange old man at the bottom
wants to take her for a ride
as she slips and she tumbles the orange man mumbles
the pennies drop down from the sky
she could say that her friend the american are
but she'd know it was a lie
she's a quarter way down and her skirts rewinded
and her little girl cheeks start to wrinkle
her smile is wide and her lips are pressed
her hair growing long and her hips
getting larger, just getting brighter, her arms
she is half the way down but the orangeman
man is impatient he tips at his watch chain
today she'll be late, but she's coming
d who taught the fingers of the little girl
            on the swingset?
as she starts to draw nearer the
view becomes clearer the splinters are painful
but she talks to Earl & the pennies
were loaded and as they exploded she
starts to spin out & around
her eyes are now closing

SLIDE

Music and Lyrics by
Amanda Palmer

SLOW + EVEN, HAUNTING

A late A-pril day and it's sun-ny out-side and a red lit-tle girl's at the top of the slide and an

or-ange old man at the bot-tom wants to take her for a ride. As she

LIKE A BATTLE MARCH----

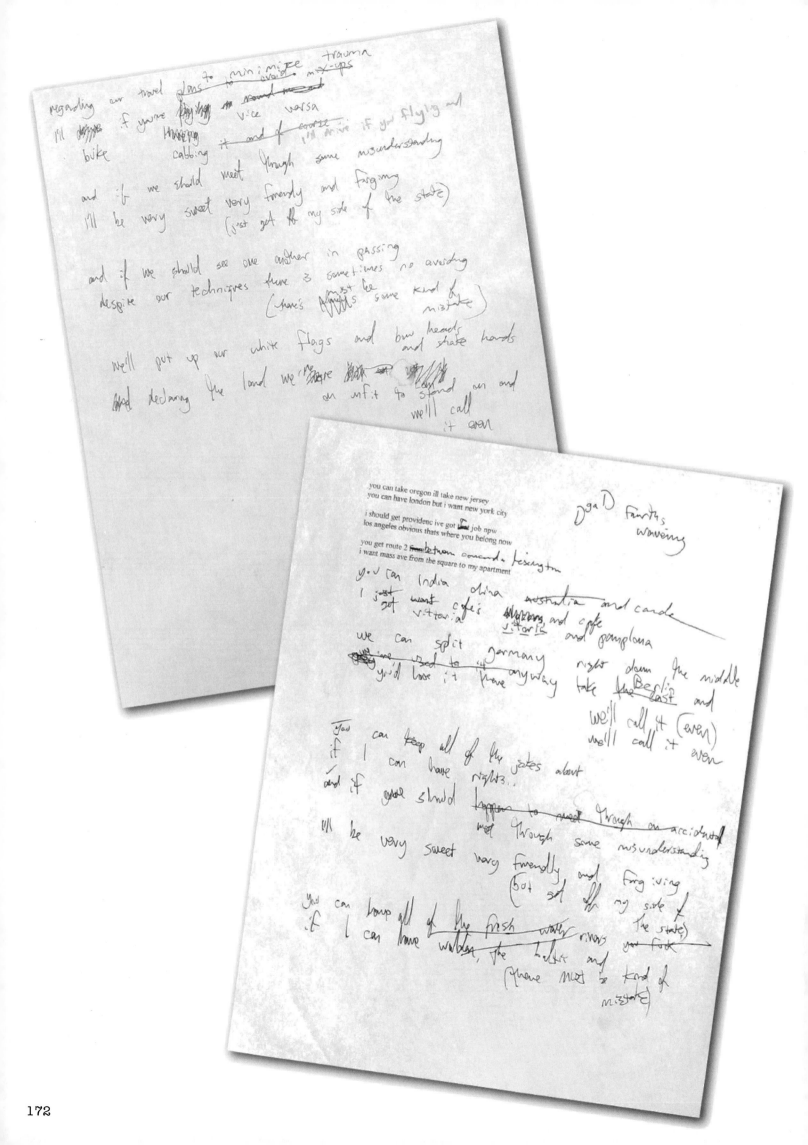

regarding our travel plans to minimize trauma / avoid mix-ups
I'll ~~~~ if you're ~~~~ vice versa
bike   cabbing it and of ~~course~~ i'll arrive if you flying and
and if we should meet through some misunderstanding
I'll be very sweet very friendly and forgiving
(just get to my side of the state)

and if we should see one another in passing
despite our techniques there's sometimes no avoiding
(there's ~~~~ must be some kind of mistake)

we'll put up our white flags and bow heads and shake hands
and declare the land we're ~~~~ an unfit to stand on and
we'll call it even

you can take oregon ill take new jersey
you can have london but i want new york city

i should get providenc ive got the job npw
los angeles obvious thats where you belong now

you get route 2 ~~lexton~~ concord. lexington
i want mass ave from the square to my apartment

(gadD fourths wavering)

you can India china ~~australia~~ and canada
I just want cafe's ~~~~ and cafe
victoria vittoria and pamplona

we can split germany right down the middle
~~~~ you'd lose it anyway take ~~the~~ Berlin east and
we'll call it (even)
we'll call it even

You can keep all of the states about
if I can have rights..
and if you should ~~happen to meet through an accidental~~
met through some misunderstanding
I'll be very sweet very friendly and forgiving
(but get to my side of the states)

you can keep all of the fresh ~~water~~ rivers you fuck
if I can have ~~waters~~, the lakes and
(there must be kind of mistake)

Acknowledgements

I would first and foremostly like to thank the Cloud Club Foundation and Lee Barron for the wonderful physical and metaphysical space he has created for me to do this work. Without him, I can't imagine where I'd (quite literally) be.

Bri Olsen, harbinger of joy to the world, helped me out early on with image scanning and gathering. Howie Kenty has worked tirelessly on transcribing these notes from ear to page and deserves huge kudos, as does Murray Barg, who helped me with his wonderful piano-playing, feedback and guidance.

I would like to thank the many voices on theshadowbox.net, who gave me early ideas and suggestions about this book. Wes Bockley and Pat Maguire have both been more than patient with me. Thanks be to JSR. I'd like to thank Emily White: Girl Friday of The Dresden Dolls, true lover of music, and Orchestrator of All Mundane Things. Without her day-to-day help, I would flail helplessly. Also huge thanks to our manager, Mike Luba and to Bart Dahl & the folks at Madison House, who Make Our Band Go.

Thanks also to Bill H, who helped proof-read and provided feedback, and whose love for my music sustains me more than he knows. Many thanks also to Ms. Becca Rosenthal, who, through taking Rock Star Energy Drink intravenously, was able to find typos that I missed and for to correct my grammar bad. Thanks also to Noah for being my main Mac Man. You do da ting good. I offer deep thanks and flash my underwear at Michael Pope and Wojtek Gwiazda.

My parents, John and Kathy, are as supportive as it gets and for that I consider myself one of the luckiest daughters in the world.

And my beautiful friend, my drummer, my musical soul mate, Brian Viglione, who supports me in more ways than I can ever know . . . he deserves thanks for helping me create this book, for selecting photos into the dawn, for helping me lose my mind and for helping me again to find it. The record album and this book would not have made it into the world without him. I love you, Brian Viglione.

Most of all, I'd like to thank my Main Editor and True Friend, Dr. C. Anthony Martignetti. Not only did he edit every draft of this book alongside me, but it was his encouragement, understanding and love that made this songwriter possible. For that there are no words or songs enough.